Designed for Joy

DESIGNED FOR JOY

How the Gospel Impacts
Men and Women,
Identity and Practice

EDITED BY
JONATHAN PARNELL
AND OWEN STRACHAN

FOREWORD BY
JOHN PIPER

CROSSWAY

WHEATON, ILLINOIS

Designed for Joy: How the Gospel Impacts Men and Women, Identity and Practice

Copyright © 2015 by Desiring God

Published by Crossway
    1300 Crescent Street
    Wheaton, Illinois 60187

Cover design: Jeff Miller, Faceout Studio

Cover image: Shutterstock

First printing 2015

Printed in the United States of America

Unless otherwise indicated, Scripture quotations are from the ESV® Bible (The Holy Bible, English Standard Version®), copyright © 2001 by Crossway, a publishing ministry of Good News Publishers. Used by permission. All rights reserved.

Scripture references marked NIV are taken from The Holy Bible, New International Version®, NIV®. Copyright © 1973, 1978, 1984, 2011 by Biblica, Inc.™ Used by permission. All rights reserved worldwide.

All emphases in Scripture quotations have been added by the authors or editors.

Trade paperback ISBN: 978-1-4335-4925-0
ePub ISBN: 978-1-4335-4928-1
PDF ISBN: 978-1-4335-4926-7
Mobipocket ISBN: 978-1-4335-4927-4

Library of Congress Cataloging-in-Publication Data

Designed for joy: how the gospel impacts men and women, identity and practice / edited by Jonathan Parnell and Owen Strachan; foreword by John Piper.
    pages cm
    Includes bibliographical references and index.
    ISBN 978-1-4335-4925-0 (tp)
    1. Sex role—Religious aspects—Christianity. 2. Sex role—Biblical teaching. 3. Men (Christian theology) 4. Women—Religious aspects—Christianity. 5. Men (Christian theology)—Biblical teaching. 6. Women—Biblical teaching. I. Parnell, Jonathan, 1985–II. Strachan, Owen.
BT708.D475   2015
233'.5—dc23   2014044856

To John Piper and Wayne Grudem

Contents

Foreword

I asked to write this foreword. I had hoped to endorse this book and help spread the word through Twitter. But then I took a PDF on the plane to Brazil and could not put it down. So I told Marshall Segal, one of the authors, who told the editors, "If you'll take me, I'd like to write the foreword."

The reason for my eagerness is partly nostalgia, partly thankfulness, partly amazement, partly admiration, and partly hope.

The editors and most of the authors of this book were not yet teenagers when Wayne Grudem and I were editing "the big blue book" called *Recovering Biblical Manhood and Womanhood* from 1988 to 1991. So to see this project emerge twenty-five years later with a shared and refined vision is like seeing our baby graduate from college. But of course, my nostalgia is no reason for you to read the book. So let's turn to what matters more.

Rising in me, as I read, was a high sense of thankfulness to God for the insight, wisdom, giftedness, biblical faithfulness, and courage of these younger authors. The vision of manhood and womanhood they are trumpeting is biblical, beautiful, and sadly obnoxious to many in society. That is, it fits with faith in Christ and infuriates those who love the atmosphere of self-actualizing autonomy—what editor Owen Strachan calls "narcissistic optimistic deism." So I am thankful for the valor of these men and women, who are willing to swim against unbiblical currents.

My amazement is that decades into this struggle, there is such a widespread and robust embrace of the beautiful biblical vision of complementary manhood and womanhood. This may strike you as an evidence of small faith on my part. Perhaps it is. But if you had tasted the vitriol of our audiences in the 1970s and 1980s, you might understand.

In the late seventies, we were called "obscene" for suggesting that God's Word taught distinct, complementary roles for men and women based on manhood and womanhood, not just competency. Therefore, the breadth and maturity and creativity and joyfulness of the complementarian crowd today triggers happy amazement in me.

Then, when I turned to these actual chapters, I read in admiration. These folks are not only good thinkers and faithful interpreters of the Bible; they are also gifted writers. The reading was not just informative and inspiring; it was a pleasure. I love to think of what these men and women will be writing in thirty years. If it's this good now, what will it be then?

Finally, I come away with hope. I am pushing to the end of my seventh decade. So I think a lot these days about what is in place for the advance of God's saving purposes on the earth in the decades to come. Reading these voices gives me hope that God is wonderfully at work to exalt his great name long after I am gone.

I commend this book to you and pray that the beauty of the vision, and the courage to speak it, will spread—for the supremacy of God in all things, for the joy of all peoples through Jesus Christ.

John Piper
Founder and Teacher
desiringGod.org

Introduction

How Does the Gospel Shape Manhood and Womanhood?

Owen Strachan

The lips of the young woman quivered. Tears rolled down her face. Her angry father stared at her. "I thought you were the kind of girl who didn't get into this sort of trouble," he said. She looked back at him, confused and adrift: "I guess I don't really know what kind of girl I am."

This exchange came in *Juno*, a poignant film made a few years ago. It's a quick scene, but it has stuck with me ever since. In this young woman's reply, I heard the confusion of an entire generation. So many young men and young women don't know who they are. They've never been taught what a man or a woman is. They may have seen terrible pain in their home, and they may have grown up without a father, or less commonly, without a mother. Or they might have had a father and a mother, but their home was compromised by sin in some way. The family didn't eat together. The parents weren't happy together. The children grew up without discipleship or investment.

This is 2015. Families are struggling. As one would expect, many young men and young women lack a road map—a script—for their lives. When you're in this confusing and confused state, you don't have answers to the most basic questions about your life. This is true of your fundamental identity, which includes your manhood or womanhood. What do I mean by this?

You Need to Know Who You Are

Many high schoolers, college students, and twentysomethings know they have a body (this is kind of obvious); further, they know they're a boy or a girl, a man or a woman; and they know they want to follow Jesus. But they have little sense of how these realities intertwine. They don't know what their gender, their sexuality, is *for*. So they're tentative. They're confused. Quietly, perhaps with some shame, they ask these kinds of questions in their own minds:

- What is my purpose?
- Why do I have this body?
- What does it mean to be a man or a woman?

This book is intended to help you figure out who you were made to be. We want to give you an inspiring vision for your life as a young man or a young woman. We see that our society is training you to think wrongly about gender and sexuality. It's telling you things like: there are no essential differences between men and women; you can change your gender if you want, and that's totally fine; you can be attracted to whomever comes most naturally to you—boys can like boys, girls can like girls; and finally, there are no responsibilities or callings that come with being a man or a woman—you do whatever you like.

In this book, we're going to show that these ideas are false and harmful. We're going to offer true words and biblical counsel to you so you can know who you are and what you were created for.

We will see that we are designed by God, and that his design brings us joy.

We're not going to simply offer you "Ten Tips to Be the Manly Man's Man, the Manliest of Them All" or "Five Ways to Make Doilies and Sing Nineteenth-Century Hymns at the Same Time." We're coming at all this from a fresh perspective. You can almost hear the can cracking open as you read these words. We want you to see that the gospel, the good news of Jesus's saving death and life-giving resurrection, is the central fact, the most important part, of your life as a God-loving man or woman. The gospel saves us, remakes us, and helps us understand who we truly are and what we are called to be for God's glory and our joy.

The gospel is what frees us from our sin. The gospel is what allows us to live to the full, our hearts soaring, our pulses pounding, our lives stretching before us, full of hope, full of meaning. With this in our minds, let's now consider four ways that the gospel shapes us as men and women.

The Gospel Makes Sense of the Image of God

One of the foundational realities of human beings, men and women alike, is that we are made in the image of God. See Genesis 1:26–27, which reads:

> Then God said, "Let us make man in our image, after our likeness. And let them have dominion over the fish of the sea and over the birds of the heavens and over the livestock and over all the earth and over every creeping thing that creeps on the earth."
>
> So God created man in his own image,
>   in the image of God he created him;
>   male and female he created them.

In other words, we're created in a special way to display the full-orbed grandeur of our Creator. We do this by creating, by thinking, by taking dominion, and by enjoying relationships with one another.

But even this awe-inspiring theological truth can be a bit abstract, can't it? What role, we might wonder, do our bodies have to play in being the image of God?

Before we're converted, we understand that we are either male or female. That's well and good. But it's only when we're saved by the grace of almighty God that we truly begin to grasp the meaning of our bodies, our sexuality. We are created as men or as women to inhabit our manhood and womanhood to the glory of our Maker. He did not make us all the same. He loves diversity. He revels in it. He created a world that pulses with difference, that explodes with color, that includes roaring waterfalls and self-inflating lizards and rapt, at-attention meerkats. But humankind, man and woman, is the pinnacle of his creation.

In Christ, we understand that our manhood or womanhood is not incidental. It's not unimportant. It is the channel through which we will give God glory all our days. We have been put here to "image" God. After conversion, we understand that we're here to give evidence of his greatness. We do that in substantial part by receiving our God-given sexuality as a gift. God created us as "male and female," not as something else. The passage above states three separate times that God "created" the man and woman, stressing God's role in making the man and woman his image bearers. There is intentionality, wisdom, and purpose in the creation of Adam and Eve, as the gospel frees us to see.

Simply receiving and reveling in this reality is a matter of worship. It's not complicated, but it is profound. *I am a man or a woman designed in just this way by God*, we should think to ourselves as we consider the body given us from above. *In the same way that the Grand Canyon was created to show God's power, and the skies his handiwork, as a man or a woman I was formed to display the beauty of his brilliant design.* In our fallenness, we're tempted to think that we have no greater reason to live, and that we're only "dust in the wind," as the famous song says. In truth, we are diamonds in the wilderness. We're no genetic accident, no freakish outcome of history. We're the special creation of God.

You could sum these thoughts up like this: as believers, we're not Christian Teletubbies. We're not gospel blobs. We're not the redeemed androgynous. We are gospel-captivated *men* and gospel-captivated *women*. When converted, we come to understand that our bodies are given us as vessels by which to put God's wisdom and intelligence and love on display.

Whether single or married, whether young or old, we have been given our manhood or womanhood as a blessing. Our bodies, with their distinctive designs, tell us that there is an exhilarating intelligence, and a grander story, behind our frame and form.

The Gospel Gives Us Power over Our Natural Weaknesses

The gospel is our fundamental marker of identity. The work of Christ applied to our hearts is such an unstoppable, unopposable force that it refigures us entirely. It's as if our old boundary markers have completely fallen away, as Paul says: "For as many of you as were baptized into Christ have put on Christ. There is neither Jew nor Greek, there is neither slave nor free, there is no male and female, for you are all one in Christ Jesus" (Gal. 3:27–28). This text doesn't mean that the gospel wipes out manhood and womanhood. It *does* mean that our fundamental reality in life is our identity in Jesus Christ.

This has immense practical value for us. As men and women, we might be tempted toward certain stereotypes. Some young men might think that being a man means bench-pressing 250 pounds, dunking a basketball, or fighting off bears with their bare hands in their spare time. (Actually, if you do that, you are pretty manly.) Some young women might think that being a woman means being sexually desirable, a lover of literature, and having a certain image. Both groups can know that we are easily tempted to find our manly and womanly identity in stereotypes. The gospel is bad news for our stereotypes. It tells us that men are self-sacrificial leaders, and that women are fearless followers of Christ.

We're going to be pulled as men and women toward certain ungodly behaviors. Men today are told that they are idiots, little boys who never grow up. We see such immaturity in Adam's initial failure to protect the woman God gave him. We also see his selfishness in his move to blame Eve for eating the forbidden fruit (Gen. 3:1–7, 12). Men are tempted by an array of sins, but they must know that the gospel is the dread foe of their laziness, selfishness, irresponsibility, and immaturity. The leaders of Scripture do not look kindly on immaturity. "Show yourself a man," David says to Solomon (1 Kings 2:2). We men hear this call today. We recognize that Jesus has the same challenge for us—and has all the grace we need to meet it.

Women today are told that their value is in their looks, or their social skills, or their ability to dominate men. We see such a desire in Eve's being deceived by the serpent and her post-fall desire to "rule over" her husband (Gen. 3:16). This is an ancient problem with modern consequences. Women are told today that they will find fulfillment and lasting happiness in being strong. They are urged to use their sexuality as a tool of empowerment. They are challenged to disdain femininity. Christian women will feel these and other temptations pull at them, but they must know that the gospel shows us a better way. It opens a door to a happier world, a world of joy. In Christ, the power of sin is overcome and the distinct beauty of womanhood is celebrated.

The world gives us false visions of happy manhood and fulfilled womanhood. It's like the dinner plate that looked so good on your friend's Instagram but tastes so bad on your plate. Selfish manhood and "fierce" womanhood are not too big for us, though; these visions of our lives are too small. Sin always looks like a monster but ends up like a mouse. It has no power over us. It has no hold on us. We don't cower in the face of the world's temptations. We laugh at them.

We scorn the principalities and powers of this age. *You think lust and power are going to entice me?* we say. *Your vision of happiness is too small. Show me a picture of my life as a man or a woman that echoes into eternity and you'll have my attention.* In Christ, we have found something better than all the world throws at us. In him, we become the men or women we were designed to be.

The Gospel Shows Us the Goodness of Limits

I remember going to basketball camp as a youngster. Part of the expectation of basketball camp is that you will hear at least one speech per week telling you that if you just practice enough, you can be the next LeBron.

You may never have dribbled a basketball, but chances are you have heard something similar. We've all been told this kind of message over and over and over again: "You are amazing. You are a star! You can be whatever you want! There are no limits in life for you." Many of us have heard of this formulation so many times that it's second nature to us. We naturally assume it's true.

This kind of thinking is embedded in modern culture. It's not just a cheesy mantra, though. It's a spiritual system in its own right. In my book *Risky Gospel*, I even give it a name: "narcissistic optimistic deism." I think this is the new "moralistic therapeutic deism." The basic view of narcissistic optimistic deism is this:

- Life is fundamentally about me.
- I deserve for life to get better and to allow me to achieve all my dreams.
- God exists to bless me and make my dreams come true.

If this sounds like a Disneyfied Christianity, that's because it is. All that's missing is a little flying insect with a magic wand. A major outcome of this way of thinking is this: you end up believing that you don't have any limits, and that if someone suggests that you do, that's a bad thing. People who might offer constructive criticism are in reality "haters." They're in the wrong, and you're in the right, because if your heart feels it and wants it, it must be good.

This perspective is disastrous for our spiritual health. It fails to account for our fallenness, our inherent sinfulness, which means that every part of us has been corrupted by the fall of Adam (see Isa. 64:6; Rom. 3:10–18). This perspective has influenced the way many people look at their bodies and lives. They say, "I can be whatever I want to be." Being a man or a woman doesn't end up meaning anything. There's no structure or order to life.

There are many outworkings of this problem. If a couple is married and the man doesn't feel like working, then he stays home. If the wife doesn't really want to spend much time with her kids, she doesn't. If a teenage boy feels like a woman, then he's free to embrace womanliness. If a twentysomething woman is attracted to other women, then she should act on that instinct. Narcissistic optimistic deism tells us that whatever we want to do or be, that's great. God is the great cheerleader in the sky. No matter what we do, he's for us. He endorses all our appetites and commends all our instincts.

This view has as much to do with the biblical God as cronuts do with Genghis Khan. Too many people today tragically follow a fairy tale god. The God of Scripture is not our life coach. He is our *Lord*. We're used to this word as Christians, and so it loses its edge. This divine title signifies that God is our master. He is our sovereign. He is our ruler. He sets the tone for right and wrong. He calls us to account for our sin.

His gospel brings both bad news and good news. It informs us that we are sinful and destined for eternal judgment (Rev. 20:14). It calls us to be re-created (Col. 3:1–10). Our chief need is not affirmation but Christ-powered transformation (Rom. 12:1–2). When it comes to our sexuality, we have God-appointed limits. These limits are not bad; they are good, and good for us. Men are called to be men. Women are called to be women. We are not free to choose our sexual predilections. We do not have the authority to remake our gender.

The gospel opens our eyes to the goodness of our manhood and womanhood, and the corresponding beauty of living according to God's design. We are not exhilarated by breaking free from God's wise and life-giving limits. When Adam and Eve failed to listen to God by disobeying his commands and ignoring their divinely mandated boundaries, they fell, and we all fell with them (Gen. 3:1–7). It was not life that came through their recklessness, but death.

Everywhere around us our culture celebrates rebellion and narcissistic willfulness. The Scripture calls us to something better, and this call envelops all our identity, including our manliness or womanliness. Don't try to become something you're not. Embrace who God made you to be, and what he calls you to be in his Word. That, and not the selfish creeds of a Disneyfied age, is where you will find true happiness and true liberation.

The Gospel Unlocks Joy for Men and Women

Sometimes, when Christians talk about embracing biblical gender roles, we're heard as only wanting people to do what's right. Let us make this clear: above all, we complementarians want to be godly men and godly women who experience the joy that comes from knowing God and living under his Word.

When you're saved, you no longer see any area of life as a burden. You see all of it as a garden of delight. Everything before you presents an opportunity to give praise and honor to your Creator and Savior (1 Cor. 10:31). This extends, in fact, even to what you eat and drink—in other words, to the most basic parts of your daily existence! That's incredible.

This helps us make sense of how we are to live as men and women. We know now that as blood-bought believers, we have the opportunity to magnify God's greatness and goodness as men and women. Our sexuality, then, is not incidental. It's not unimportant. It's not a curse that we want to get rid of. It's not a burden that God has given us that we do everything we can to downplay. Our manhood and womanhood is a God-designed pathway to delight.

Our sexuality wasn't designed by a secular entrepreneur, a victimizing pornographer, or a Jason Bourne wannabe. Manhood was produced by the spectacular intelligence of the Father. Womanhood was created by the cosmic brilliance of the Father. Our culture tells us the opposite: "Sure, you may be born with a few certain parts, but that doesn't mean anything. Men and women are interchangeable. Gender is malleable, changeable, unfixed, unimportant." This is the opposite of the biblical witness. God made Adam as a man. Then God made Eve, an image bearer like Adam as a human being, but unlike him as a woman. She had a purpose in creation: to be his "helper," a noble title befitting a high calling (Gen. 2:18).

When Yahweh brought Eve to Adam, the man did not glumly nod his head in acknowledgment. He exploded with praise and delight:

Then the man said,

"This at last is bone of my bones
   and flesh of my flesh;
she shall be called Woman,
   because she was taken out of Man." (Gen. 2:23)

If this is read in church, it's probably read flatly, without a lot of emphasis. In reality, the whole section should be in ALL CAPS. The man "at last" has his covenantal partner. He is lonely no longer; he has a helpmate; he finds the woman unlike him, fearfully and wonderfully made, and this difference thrills him and causes him to shout praise to his Maker.

The body, we see, is good. Manhood is good. Womanhood is good. We don't all look the same according to our sex. Not every man has thick shoulders and a lantern jaw. Not every woman has a certain figure and lustrous locks. But whatever we look like, we all give immense glory to God simply by living joyfully as men or as women, savoring our divine design, seizing opportunities (as later chapters discuss) to live obediently as followers of Christ according to our sex and our foundational Christian calling.

This is why we're here. This is what the complementarian movement, bursting with life, is all about. This is our hope and prayer for you: that in owning your manhood and womanhood and viewing it through the clarifying lens of the gospel, you would give God much glory, and experience much joy.

Refigured Identity

I want to leave you with a true story that pulls together much of what we've covered here. It's a story of a little boy whose body was weak. He couldn't walk, and he was carried everywhere he went. Over time, he became needy and weepy. If you saw him, you would have pitied him. He was not even ten years of age, and he was already way behind.

But then something happened. The little boy was adopted by a Christian family. This was no ordinary family, however. It was one led by a godly father, a man whose blend of kindness and authority drew respect from his wife and children. His wasn't the ultra-modern home you see on Hulu nowadays—teens eye-rolling, chaos reigning, Dad zoned out on his iPhone, Mom trying to tame the far-past-gone toddlers. This was a home where a father trained and pastored his children, and a mother devoted herself to her kids. This was a home where you were expected to pull your weight, pursue maturity, and sacrifice your interests to those of others.

This was the home the little boy entered. He couldn't have articulated his feelings, but he knew something was different. There was order. There was discipline. And there was love, abundant love, that spilled out into laughter and playing and real conversation. But the boy wasn't the only one watching. The father was watching, too. He thought to himself, *This boy isn't lame. He's not gonna be a track star. But I think he can walk.*

After a couple of days, he decided not to keep these thoughts to himself. He gently prodded the little boy, his new son, to try walking. So the boy did. At first it didn't go well. Walking wasn't supposed to happen. His self-identity was fixed. But then something clicked. The boy took one step, then another. A lurch became a walk. Pretty soon he, too, was caught up in the whirl of the home. He wasn't the fastest, and the other kids had to help him at times. But the switch was back on. The boy had come alive. His strength was bigger than his weakness. His identity was refigured.

This true story elegantly illustrates what happens when the gospel speaks into our sexuality. We gain strength from the power of Christ's redemptive work to become who we were made by God to be. Once we were weak; now, in the Spirit, we are strong.

Once, like the young woman in *Juno*, we didn't know what kind of man or woman we are. We didn't know what our manhood or womanhood was *for*. Now, in Christ, we understand. Now, like a child taking his first faltering steps, we are free to walk. Now, in Christ, we are free to run.

1

Being a Man and Acting Like One

Jonathan Parnell

Paul writes to the leaders in the church at Corinth, "Be watchful, stand firm in the faith, act like men, be strong. Let all that you do be done in love" (1 Cor. 16:13–14). When Paul says to "act like men," he means something different from "act like women." There is actually a word for it in the original Greek—*andrizomai*—literally meaning "behave like a man." The only place it shows up throughout the New Testament is here in 1 Corinthians 16.

As the context and classical use suggest, the idea has to do with courage and bravery. To "act like men"—or "be courageous," as the NIV puts it—is to act in a way that is somehow different from a boy, in terms of maturity, and is somehow different from a woman, in terms of gender. As Paul shows us, masculinity—to act like men—is something that fits with standing firm and being strong. And standing firm and being strong fits with masculinity. The connection is apparently so natural that the words are synonyms. So what is that? What does it mean to act like men—to be masculine?

Getting to the Who

Actually, before we get to the understanding of what it means to act like men, we need to know *who*, most generally, *should* act like men. The obvious answer here is that men should act like men, but the qualification "most generally" is important. There are instances when both men *and* women are called to exhibit masculine traits, just as there are instances when both men *and* women should exhibit feminine traits. In fact, the healthiest examples of humans are those who know how to employ either traits when different circumstances require them.

Paul models this for us in his letter to the churches in Thessalonica. He describes his ministry: "We were gentle among you, like a nursing mother taking care of her own children" (1 Thess. 2:7). And then, "Like a father with his children, we exhorted each one of you and encouraged you and charged you to walk in a manner worthy of God" (1 Thess. 2:11–12). Nursing and exhorting, tenderness and toughness—the apostle Paul's ministry featured two different characteristics commonly associated with two different genders. Sometimes men and women need to be strong and stand firm (i.e., act like men), and sometimes men and women need to be gentle and nurturing (i.e., act like a mother). Neither masculinity nor femininity is *exclusively* tied to maleness or femaleness, though masculine traits are most generally (and appropriately) associated with men, and feminine with women.

Understanding True Manhood

With that said, it is this most general association of masculinity that is worth more thought. It is obvious to most of us that men are most naturally called to exhibit masculine traits. But *who* are men? What does it mean to *be* a man? Apart from what we do, what is a man in the most basic, God-given sense?

This is an important question because only the combination of *being* a man and *acting* like one constitutes *true* manhood. This is the equation at the heart of this chapter. There are two essential parts:

1. The divinely ordained fact of being a man (maleness)
2. The man's derivative behavior of acting like men (masculinity)

Both of these parts are necessary to realize true manhood: God gives maleness in his creative design for man; men cultivate masculinity as our behavior in response to that creative design. In other words, maleness + masculinity = true manhood.

If we skip immediately to behavior, to the characteristics of masculinity without some understanding of male identity, then we run the risk of truncating manhood as mainly about what we do, and therefore leave room for the misunderstanding that manhood is a lifestyle option rather than something built into our being by our Creator.

So first we ask, what is maleness? Because then, after considering what it means to be a man, can we most responsibly ask what it means to act like one and thus understand mature manhood. Or for starters, and more foundational to both questions, we need a real sense of why it even matters.

Why It Matters

It matters what a man is and how he acts because that says something about the God who made him. This is key to any thinking about ourselves. Our existence is a lot bigger than the little you and me to whom we are most accustomed. If we fail to understand this, if we short-circuit our minds and move straight to the perfunctory details, we'll simply go on puzzling ourselves over hollow implications drawn from the wrong starting place. We shouldn't jump ahead to roles without knowing why. There is more for us to see.

God created us for himself—to behold, and be happy in, the manifold perfections of his character displayed in Jesus Christ, his perfect image. He spoke us into existence to join him in the gladness of his Son, the radiance of his glory (Heb. 1:3), and then reflect that same radiance with our lives. All the details of this universe are hardwired toward this end, including the corn and grits of manhood. What makes men *men*, or women *women*, is intrinsically connected to the majesty of the God in our design. We each exist as we do in order to display that glory. Which means, when it comes to understanding "man," how we *see* God is more important than knowing what we're supposed to do.

And it's actually here, in beholding the glory of God, in seeing Jesus, that we experience our deepest joy and learn how to live. We were made for this. In fact, because understanding what a man *is* and *does* is ultimately about God's glory, it is simultaneously about human flourishing, because only God's glory can truly satisfy the human heart. God's goal in manhood and womanhood is that we would know him, and in knowing him, be forever glad in all that he is for us in Christ.

So now, upon this foundation, we step into what might be the densest part of this book. By way of disclaimer, in view of the shorter, more practical chapters to follow, this chapter might feel like a trip down to the boiler room—looking less pretty and requiring more work—but hopefully filling the rest of these pages with heat. Here goes.

What Does It Mean to Be a Man?

God created humans in his image—"male and female he created them" (Gen. 1:27). The Genesis account says it straightforward. There is the human being, brought into existence by God as the pinnacle of his creation and bestowed with an unparalleled dignity. We have dominion over the rest of creation. We bear God's image. And there are two kinds of us: male and female. That's the way it is, and God said it was *good*.

So much of what it means to be one and not the other—to be male, not female; or female, not male—is left to natural theology. The Bible doesn't tell us about chromosomes, and it doesn't need to. In those instances when anatomy is the topic, Scripture doesn't make the case for our differences but assumes that we already know them (as is so clear in Song of Solomon). Scripture's virtual silence on these specifics suggests that we understand it naturally. And therefore, because the mechanics of maleness are so generally intuitive, the brief explanation of maleness here will draw from the natural revelation common to us all, which the Bible implies and ultimately enlightens. This natural revelation can be considered in three aspects: *the observable world, human society,* and *human interaction with the world.*[1]

Using these three perspectives to view the reality of natural revelation, we can focus more closely on sexuality through a similar grid, examining sexuality from the three vantages of *sex, gender,* and *gender identity.* These categories provide a natural lens through which to understand what it means to be a man.[2] Sex is biological, recognized in the observable world; gender is sociological, recognized in the perceptions of masculinity and femininity in human society; and gender identity is psychological, recognized as an individual's personal interaction with the observable world within human society.[3]

Biological Perspective

The first perspective is biological. It is something that we cannot choose, but rather is given us by God. Therefore, this perspective regulates the others. It refers to our chromosomal makeup expressed in the anatomy. Put in the simplest terms, the male anatomy is different from the female anatomy. I hope that doesn't shock you. Undeniably, this biological difference is part of the observable world.

---

[1] Alister McGrath, *The Open Secret: A New Vision for Natural Theology* (Oxford: Blackwell, 2008), 126ff. By way of a distinctively Christian explanation of natural theology, McGrath writes, "A Christian natural theology rests on the premise that, although nature may be publicly observable, *the key to its proper interpretation is not given within the natural order itself*" (139, emphasis added). This is to say, though nature in these three aspects (observable world, society, reason) is helpful in regard to understanding maleness, the correct interpretation of the natural order requires that the human interpreter, within the confines of culture, has his or her intellect controlled by the miraculous, particular revelation of God. This means we try to see as much as we can in what's there, but Scripture is always the final authority.

[2] These categories are introduced by Kevin Vanhoozer as a case study on how to do theology in Walter C. Kaiser Jr. et al., *Four Views on Moving beyond the Bible to Theology* (Grand Rapids: Zondervan, 2009). He cites two resources on this topic: Justin Edward Tanis, *Trans-Gendered: Theology, Ministry, and Communities of Faith,* Center for Lesbian and Gay Studies in Religion and Ministry (Cleveland: Pilgrim, 2003), and *Transsexuality: A Report by the Evangelical Alliance Policy Commission* (Carlisle, UK: Paternoster, 2000).

[3] Vanhoozer calls these the "chromosomal marker," the "cultural marker," and the "consciousness marker" (*Four Views,* Kindle locations 3251–54).

By the simplest inspection, we can identify the differences between being a male and being a female, and we often operate based upon these observations.

In the early weeks of my wife's first pregnancy, we jumped headfirst into the exciting task of finding a name for our child. We scoured books and websites and even took a weekend trip with the sole purpose of landing on a name—*two* names, actually. See, we weren't sure yet if we were expecting a boy or a girl. Our plan was to choose two names, but let the twenty-week ultrasound "make" the final decision. What we were going to call this child was ultimately up to not what name we thought sounded best or had the most meaning, but what kind of child God had given us—which we could discern by looking at a certain spot of our baby's body with the help of medical technology. I remember well the nurse telling us, in a much less dramatic fashion than I had anticipated, "It's a little girl," to which I replied, "It's Elizabeth!" That was five names ago now, and each decision since has still come down to that same moment.

Males have male parts and females have female parts, and they always will, unless some unnatural inhibition occurs—in which case we are reminded that though this biological perspective is normative, the holistic picture of maleness is formed by two other perspectives.

Sociological Perspective

Second, there is the societal witness. These are the culturally conditioned characteristics that we identify with the God-given realities of maleness or femaleness. In short, this perspective shows us that there is a male way to look, walk, and talk as perceived by societies of men and women, and that when men express themselves this way, they are identified as males. Additionally, when a male doesn't correspond to this societal expectation, it is considered unnatural or strange. Every human culture is ingrained, at some level, with this binary lens of understanding itself. And though these societal markers vary among different places and times, Scripture suggests that it is right for us to abide by them as male and female, so long as they are not sinful.

Case in point, consider Paul's instructions to the first-century Corinthians when he says it is a disgrace for men to have long hair (1 Cor. 11:14). According to that culture, and our own in similar ways, there is a masculine way for men to wear their hair. Commenting on this passage, Kevin DeYoung says that Paul is making two universal statements about gender: (1) it isn't right for men to act like women; and (2) society influences the norms of masculine and feminine expression.[4]

At the most basic level, this societal witness points to the human consensus that certain actions correspond most appropriately to certain beings.

Psychological Perspective

Third, there is a psychological aspect to being a man. According to one's personal interaction with the world, males will typically perceive themselves as such. They embrace the biological and societal witness to their gender identity. Males feel male. They sense maleness in their makeup and conform to the societal perception of how that should look. In most cases, males interpret the normative perspective of male anatomy and the situational perspective of gender labels to mean, existentially, in profoundly common terms, "I am a man."

There are situations, however, when the fallen nature of our world impairs this understanding. Sometimes men may not feel like men, even if they have male anatomy and look like men. For example, transgender individuals typically claim that something is missing in the existential correspondence to their given anatomy and societal appearance. They perceive themselves differently than who they are and how they look. Sadly, these individuals grant this

---

[4] Kevin DeYoung, "Play the Man," *Journal for Biblical Manhood and Womanhood* 16, no. 2 (2011): 13. DeYoung makes the case for the general principle "The Bible teaches that men can be effeminate but that they shouldn't be." Thanks to Tony Reinke for pointing me to this article.

personal perception the ultimate authority and attempt to manipulate the other perspectives through the use of hormones and surgical procedures. Ironically, the goal of becoming transgender is to have all three perspectives saying the same thing, even if by inauthentic, superficial means.

Parts, Traits, Sense

To be sure, no one of these three perspectives testifies to our sexuality on its own, but they all work together—as three vantages on one whole—to form our identity as male or female. And that information is adequate in almost every case, even if one perspective is blurred by our sin-tainted world.

In general, to be male is to be created with male anatomy, to be considered male according to the societal perception, and to understand oneself as male in light of one's personal interaction with biology and society. Or put even more plainly, being a male is to naturally have male parts, male traits, and a male sense.

This is what it means to be a man. This reality of maleness is the fundamental aspect of manhood exclusively given to the man by God and from which the man answers the masculine call.

Defining True Manhood

The following two chapters of this book, by Joe Rigney and David Mathis, target the question of true manhood: What does it mean for *men* to *act like men*? But before we get there, I'd like to lead into that discussion by first anchoring masculinity in the most basic calling of every human: the calling to love.

Returning to 1 Corinthians 16, notice verse 14, following the string of imperatives that includes "act like men": "Be watchful, stand firm in the faith, act like men, be strong. *Let all that you do be done in love*" (vv. 13–14). "Let all that you do be done in love." The call to love is certainly not exclusive to men. It is at the heart of the two greatest commandments, where Jesus said, in essence, love God and love people (Matt. 22:37–39)—which goes for everybody.

Men and women both should love, and the question of masculinity (and femininity as we'll see) gets at precisely how that looks, distinctive to gender.

Masculinity, then, is more than how a man should act; it's an expression of a man's love. And its distinguishing feature is self-sacrificing leadership. In a phrase, masculinity is gladly assuming sacrificial responsibility.[5] Given our understanding of maleness above, combined with this description of masculinity, our working definition of true manhood goes like this: *True manhood is man's response to God's calling for men to gladly assume sacrificial responsibility.* There are three key words here worth highlighting.

First, manhood is a *response*. This is central to masculinity, which is derivative from our God-given male identity. Manhood is not one option among others for whoever is interested. It is a reality that corresponds to God's creation. It is mainly the result of *who we are*, which gives rise to *what we do*. Therefore, we should be clear that manhood itself is never self-creative. We are not making ourselves to be anything. Rather, we are responding to what God has designed. In essence, manhood is our realization, through masculine action, of our God-designed male being as witnessed in the three perspectives.

Second, manhood is accepted *gladly*. This important qualifier connects back to the point of why this all matters. Manhood can be a great burden. It is a heavy responsibility to carry, as we'll soon see. But the Christian response to this weight is not grudging acceptance, because it is full of faith. We understand that God's design for manhood has our eternal joy in view. Our journey of maturing into the character God has intended for us means that we will encounter more of his sufficiency. He will prove himself, through the gospel of his Son, to be our all-satisfying anchor and hope. Just as Jesus, "for the joy that was set before him," endured the cross (Heb. 12:2), we can be sustained through the weightiest parts of the masculine call because we rest in the deeper pleasure on the other side.

Third, manhood is about taking *responsibility*. This is another

<hr>

[5] Douglas Wilson, *Father Hunger: Why God Calls Men to Love and Lead Their Families* (Nashville: Thomas Nelson, 2012), 51–52.

way to say that manhood is about leadership.[6] Men are given a charge to lead, provide for, and protect women and children. Within the home, and even society at large, men are designed to carry the mantle of seeing into tomorrow, plotting a course in that tomorrow, and guarding that course from inhibitions. In this sense, men are essentially leaders. This, of course, does not negate the leadership capacity of women or the innumerable everyday tasks of women that demand their leadership. It only suggests that men are uniquely called by God to be the ones who step out first. And this call to lead—this charge to take responsibility—is naturally accompanied by *sacrifice*. Typically, the action of stepping out, paving a course, and fending off assailants comes at some loss to the man himself. I say "loss" in the most temporal sense—loss in terms of the Christian man saying about love's cost what missionary David Livingstone famously said: "I never made a sacrifice."

In the hardest moment of leading, manhood "takes it on the chin" and exchanges the world's lust after instant gratification for that deeper joy of finding our pleasure in the pleasure of the ones we love. It isn't easy, and none of us will be perfect, but this is what it means to "play the man"—and the raw materials we need have already been provided. Given God's grace in our Spirit-empowered practice, and learning from the godly examples around us, any man, regardless of his past failures, can grow more and more into this role. I mean that. The call to manhood is not last week, or next year, but today. And we answer the call not once upon a time, or later down the road, but here and now, by God's grace.

More than a Profile

The last thing to say about manhood before the next two chapters is perhaps the most important. We must remember that God has not

---

[6] John Piper writes, "When the Bible teaches that men and women fulfill different roles in relation to each other, charging man with a unique leadership role, it bases the differentiation not on temporary cultural norms but on permanent facts of creation" (*What's the Difference: Manhood and Womanhood Defined according to the Bible* [Wheaton, IL: Crossway, 2002], 21). Piper defines masculinity this way: "At the heart of mature masculinity is a sense of benevolent responsibility to lead, provide for, and protect women in ways appropriate to a man's differing relationships" (ibid., 22).

left us with a mere profile of manhood, but he's given us an actual Person. We have a flawless example of what true manhood looks like in the life of Jesus Christ. This example, in particular, is seen in the way he loved his bride—a way that men are commanded to emulate (Eph. 5:25).

Again, as discussed above, both men and women are called to follow the example of loving like Jesus (Eph. 5:2). But this example presents a peculiar calling to men. Paul's instructions for the Christian household in Ephesians 5 singles out the love of Jesus as the normative characteristic of a husband's relationship to his wife. A husband's love for his wife—indicative of true manhood—involves great personal sacrifice. Jesus gave himself up for his bride, and so should we—for our wives, especially, and even for the others God brings into the sphere of our love.

In this way, Jesus embodied the masculine call and stands as the great example of true manhood. If anyone ever gladly assumed sacrificial responsibility, it was Jesus. Looking to the joy that was set before him, he walked headfirst into the pain and loss of the cross and drained the cup that only he could drink. He assumed the weight of our sins on his shoulders to pave the path for a new humanity and secure our everlasting good. Jesus is the man—the true and better man—who exemplifies and empowers us to walk in his steps as each of us embraces our God-given design to be a man, and act like one.

2

Masculinity Handed Down

Joe Rigney

Masculinity is the glad assumption of sacrificial responsibility. It's our response to God's calling. In this chapter, I hope to provide a window into masculinity by referring to its most natural and practical reminder in my life, how to teach my two young sons to act like men. To do this, I'll describe seven desires I have for my boys as they grow into mature manhood.

1. I WANT MY SONS TO GROW UP TO BE TRUE MEN OF GOD— FIRST IN, LAST OUT, LAUGHING LOUDEST.

Around my house, this is our way of expressing the glad assumption of sacrificial responsibility. It's a summary of King Lune of Archenland's words about kingship in *The Horse and His Boy*: "For this is what it means to be a king: to be first in every desperate attack and last in every desperate retreat, and when there's hunger in the land (as must be now and then in bad years) to wear finer clothes and laugh louder over a scantier meal than any man in your land."[1]

---

[1] C. S. Lewis, *The Horse and His Boy*, The Chronicles of Narnia (New York: HarperCollins, 1954), 223.

Kingship (and by extension true masculinity) means being the first into the battle. If there's a danger to be faced, a true man will face it first. If there's a burden to be borne, a man will bear it first. A man will see to it that pain and hardship fall in his lap before they ever fall upon those under his care. Too many men think that male headship means making demands, getting their way, and riding around on a high horse. But godly leadership doesn't give us the right to lord our authority over others; it means, as my friend Toby Sumpter says, that it is our glory to die first.

While many of us will never be called upon to fight in a physical battle to protect our families, all of us are called to look for opportunities to be first in, last out, laughing loudest. "For even the Son of Man came not to be served but to serve" (Mark 10:45). Therefore, a man of God comes home not to be served, but to serve. After a hard day's work, a godly man enters his home, not with a list of demands, but with an eagerness to give. He comes to relieve the burdens of his wife, not add to them. He comes to play with his kids, not shunt them off to their rooms while he puts his feet up.

I want my sons to aspire to be men who give until it hurts, and whistle the while. I want them to lean into sacrifice with unconquerable laughter in their hearts. "I will most gladly spend and be spent for your souls," Paul says to the Corinthians (2 Cor. 12:15). Godly masculinity ought to be the happiest thing you ever saw. A twinkle in the eyes, a brightness in the smile, a laughter in the bones—these are the qualities of a man who has planted his feet upon a Rock and will not be shaken when the earth gives way and the waters foam (Ps. 46:1–3).

2. I WANT MY SONS TO EMBRACE THEIR CALLING AS PROTECTORS OF THE WEAK.

One of my central responsibilities as a father to my sons is to train their hands for war. At our house, swordplay is practice for life. When we don our plastic armor and foam swords, we are getting ready for real sacrifices. I want them to see that the primary burden of defense—whether of home, family, church, or country—lies with them. The world is filled with gardens, and, as one pastor says, gardens always attract serpents. Therefore, my prayer is that they put on their armor, keep their swords sharp, and play the man.

What's more, part of their training is learning to fall down and get up again. I want my boys to fall down. I want them to get skinned knees, bumped heads, and bruised arms. I want them to experience pain (in small doses) so that they learn to laugh it off. "What do we do when we fall down?" I ask. "Laugh and keep playing," they answer.

Masculinity is about taking responsibility for the physical, emotional, and spiritual safety of those in our care. For me, this means, among other things, locking the doors at night, giving hugs and kisses away as if fatherly affection were snow in a Minnesota winter, and praying for mighty angels with swords of flame to guard the bedrooms while we sleep. It means identifying threats and enemies of whatever kind and taking steps to guard and keep those entrusted to me. Most importantly, it means killing the dragon that lurks in my own heart. The greatest threat to those in my care is my own sin and rebellion. Therefore, protecting others demands a single-minded and glad-hearted pursuit of holiness.

3. I WANT MY SONS TO GLADLY SUBMIT TO LAWFUL AUTHORITY.

The prerequisite for being in authority is recognizing that one is always *under authority*. Many men think that leadership is about being "the boss," when in fact it's first and fundamentally about recognizing that God is the Boss (Eph. 6:9; Col. 4:1). Masculinity welcomes accountability, authority, and oversight. The foundation of godly manhood is cheerful obedience to lawful authority.

A man is in no position to expect obedience from others if he is not first eager to render it to those over him in the Lord. I want my boys to grow up with a deep awareness that their father is a man under authority. I want to model for them glad submission to God in his Word, to the elders of our church, to my boss at work. God is calling them to honor, respect, and obey me; therefore, I want to show them how.

The flip side of submission to lawful authority is resistance to unlawful authority. Part of teaching my sons godly obedience is helping them to grasp the differences between authority that is established by God and that which is usurped by ungodly men. And I want them to defy the latter precisely because they desire to obey the former. This means celebrating the examples of men like the apostle Peter ("We must obey God rather than men"—Acts 5:29), Martin Luther King Jr. ("An unjust law is no law at all"—quoting St. Augustine), and Robin Hood ("If an outlaw is the last available occupation for an honest man in England, then I will be an outlaw").[2]

4. I WANT MY SONS TO PRACTICE SELF-CONTROL FOR THE JOY IN IT.

Paul singles out self-control as one of the fundamental callings for young men (Titus 2:6) and old (2:2). This self-control is the result of the grace of God in the gospel (Titus 2:11–12). It is grace that trains us to renounce ungodliness and live self-controlled lives in this present age. Paul identifies self-control as a fruit of the Spirit (Gal. 5:23), which means that it is more than mere willpower. One of the fundamental aims of the Spirit of God is to restore control of me to me, so that I work out what God is working in (Phil. 2:12–13).

The Bible teaches that the glory of young men is their strength. But inactive strength is idleness and passivity, and therefore strength must be directed to some end. On the other hand, unbridled strength is reckless and dangerous, and soon causes harm and destruction. Strength governed by wisdom, strength guided by the Spirit of God, strength aimed at the good of others—this is what God is after.

For my sons, this means controlling their angers and outbursts, not collapsing into whining and fussing when they don't get their

---

[2] Jim Veiss, *A Storyteller's Version of The Three Musketeers—Robin Hood*, audio CD (Charlottesville, VA: Greathall Productions, 1999).

way, and learning the time and place to be silly, loud, and crazy. As they grow, self-control will be necessary in getting out of bed for school, completing homework before playing outside, and resisting the pull of sexual temptation.

Chesterton once remarked that the reason that order and structure exist in God's world is to make room for good things to run wild. God erects walls around the city so that life can happen inside. God establishes boundaries so that joy can be unleashed. A godly man respects and delights in the fences built by God, and then rides bareback across the bounded plain, wind whipping in his hair.

5. I WANT MY SONS TO CELEBRATE THE WONDERS OF FEMININITY.

Too often magnifying the virtues of one sex leads to the denigration of the other. But God designed masculinity and femininity to complement one another. Men and women were made to dance. And the whole point of men leading in the dance is to showcase the beauty of women.

Therefore, there can be no godly masculinity where feminine virtue is not celebrated. Godly men love the glory of women, because the woman's glory is his glory (1 Cor. 11:7). This means that in general we can measure the faithfulness of men *by the flourishing of women*. In a Christian family, the fruitfulness of the wife and children is the evidence of God's blessing on the husband. If you want to see whether biblical masculinity is present in a congregation, look to the women and children. Are they thriving? Are they cared for? Are they holy and happy and hopeful?

I want my sons to be awed by the bright strength and life-giving wisdom of women. I want them to hear their mother's praises sung by their father, in season and out of season. When I bless them at night, I want them to eagerly hope that my prayers for them come true: "May the Lord lift up his countenance upon you and give you peace, and some day a wife like your mommy." I want there to be no hint of male superiority or dominance, but only gratitude to God for the tremendous blessing of women.

6. I WANT MY SONS TO PUT TO DEATH ANY VESTIGE
OF FALSE MASCULINITY.

My boys were born as sons of Adam, which is "honor enough to erect the head of the poorest beggar, and shame enough to bow the shoulders of the greatest emperor on earth."[3] Adam was called to keep and guard the garden (just as the Levites kept and guarded the tabernacle), but instead, when the dragon approached his wife with his lying words, Adam stood there in passivity and silence. He was commanded not to eat from the forbidden tree, but when his wife offered it to him, he chose to defy his Father, to listen to her voice, and to worship the creature rather than the Creator. He was expected to take responsibility for her protection and provision, but when God called him to account for his sin, he blamed his wife, effectively demanding that God put her to death for their sin.

Passivity, idolatry, abuse. These are the hallmarks of Adamic masculinity. It is the opposite of the glad assumption of sacrificial responsibility. Instead of first in, last out, laughing loudest, we find last in, first out, and sulking all the way. I want to train my boys to recognize the old man who lives in their hearts and to take up their cross and put him to death daily.

I'm under no illusions that Adamic masculinity will be utterly destroyed in this life. But there can be progress, and we must begin where the first Adam last failed: with responsibility and repentance. When I counsel newly married men, I remind them that in a marriage of sinners, conflict is inevitable. Some say that love means never having to say that you're sorry. For a godly husband, love means that you have the privilege of saying you're sorry first.

7. I WANT MY SONS TO SEE JESUS CHRIST AS THE
GROUND AND GOAL OF THEIR MASCULINITY.

Christ is the ground of our masculinity. He took Adamic humanity into the grave with him and emerged with a new way to be human

---

[3] C. S. Lewis, *Prince Caspian: The Return to Narnia*, The Chronicles of Narnia (n.p.: HarperCollins, n.d.), Kindle edition, locations 2270–71.

and a renewed way of being a man. Unlike Adam, Christ killed the dragon to get the girl. And he killed the dragon by dying himself. When he saw his bride heading down the broad road to destruction, what did he do? He didn't blame, he bled. He didn't damn, he died. He didn't gripe and grumble and groan. Instead he gladly and graciously gave himself up for her, that he might purify and beautify his bride.

Christ died for the sins of Adam and all the sons who follow in his steps, that he might make a way for us to return to our Father and recover our royal calling. The gospel of Jesus Christ is the only hope for failed and fallen men, and it is a living and abiding hope.

My prayer for my boys (and for myself and the men who read this chapter) is that we would embrace this gospel and answer Christ's call to be his little brothers, following him into the breach, laying down our lives for others, and doing so for the joy set before us. First in, last out, laughing loudest.

3

The Happy Call to Holistic Provision

David Mathis

Lead, protect, and provide—masculinity is more than these, but not less. These three summary actions are as good as any for saying what masculinity does as the glad assumption of sacrificial responsibility.

To understand the enigmatic realities of masculinity and femininity, we find great help in the complementary relationship we were made for as husbands and wives—and Ephesians 5 is the big flashing arrow. The husband is head "as Christ is the head of the church" (v. 23). He is to love "as Christ loved the church and gave himself up for her" (v. 25). And he is to nourish and cherish his wife "as Christ does the church" (v. 29).

Make no mistake, husbands get no special privileges with Jesus by aiming to walk in the God-man's steps. Men and women are one in Christ (Gal. 3:28), fellow heirs of the grace of life (1 Pet. 3:7). The husband isn't any closer to Jesus because in the marital picture he takes his cues from Jesus, and she from the church. This headship is not one of privilege; this love, not one of ease; nor is this nourishing and cherishing born of convenience. Rather, the masculine calling echoes the one who "gave himself up for her" (Eph. 5:25). It is not the position of one being waited on, hand and foot, but of one stooping to his knees to wash her feet and shoulder the cross beam on the way to Calvary.

At first blush, it may sound honoring to a man to hear that his path has been pioneered by the Savior himself. But on any good second thought, a man realizes that this is a great burden to bear. The honest Christian who has looked the calling of true masculinity in the face will say with the apostle, "Who is sufficient for these things?" (2 Cor. 2:16).

Perhaps it's a good thing that most men don't know what they're getting into when they ask for a woman's hand in marriage. Whether or not a man realizes it when he takes his vows and makes the covenant, soon he must discover—hopefully sooner than later—that gaining his life in the end will mean losing it at first. He is signing up for an Easter celebration that happens only on the other side of Good Friday. As with Jesus, this headship is not for him to be served, but to serve and give his life for another (Mark 10:45). The Good Shepherd lays down his life. So must the man for his wife. There is more to masculinity than husbanding, but it forms and shapes our calling from top to bottom.

Taking Cues from Christ's Self-Sacrifice

Four times in John 10, the Shepherd from whom we take our cues gives us the outcome of his glad assumption of sacrificial responsibility. It's a death that gives way to life. But death must come first. Verse 11: "I am the good shepherd. The good shepherd lays down his life for the sheep." Verse 15: "I lay down my life for the sheep." Verse 17: "I lay down my life that I may take it up again." And verse 18: "I lay it down of my own accord." In other words, he gives his own life, and he does so with joy, looking to the greater life and abundance ahead. This is the cruciform pattern, the glad assumption of sacrificial responsibility.

Here in John 10, we catch glimpses of Jesus as leader (vv. 3–4), protector (vv. 11–13), and provider (vv. 9–10). The previous two chapters of this short volume have touched on leadership and protection. Now the task before us is provision.

Two Promises to Provide

I was standing in the same spot when I made the two most significant promises of my life. Both included the pledge to provide. First was June 29, 2007, our wedding day. In one of the weightiest moments of my life, I repeated after the pastor, and covenanted with my bride,

> And I do promise,
> before God and these witnesses,
> to be your loving and faithful husband,
> to serve you and protect you,
> to lead you and *provide* for you . . .

Then again on October 17, 2010, my wife and I stood together in that same church building, this time facing the congregation, instead of each other, with our arms full of twin boys. We pledged "to *provide*, through God's blessing, for the physical, emotional, intellectual, and spiritual needs" of our then three-month-old children.

Here is the heart of the masculine summons to provision, which shapes masculinity even when there are no wife and kids: first, to provide for the wife; then with her, to provide for the children. Both are enormous vows, beautifully fitting to our design and nearly impossible to live up to. Little did I know, as a single man in years prior, how much these two promises to provide for wife and children would shape my life in such a short span of time—and yet how deeply they would resonate with God's design in my masculine call.

Four Aspects of Provision

These two promises (to wife and to children), and these four promised provisions (physical, emotional, intellectual, and spiritual) serve well in giving shape to the masculine calling to provide. There is more to masculine provision than that of a husband and father—much more—but these roles, rightly understood, penetrate to the heart of masculinity and give us plenty of form and texture to sketch in any remaining segments.

However we structure it, there are at least two key insights we need to maintain. The first is that there's a distinctly masculine way of relating to women and children. Men are called to provide for women, and to provide, with women, for children. While men and women share in the work of providing for children, they perform this work through different roles.

The second insight, and this will structure what follows, is that we men are called to a holistic provision. One way to divide up the whole is by using the four categories mentioned above: physical, emotional, intellectual, and spiritual.

Physical

The mention of a man's provision likely sends our minds to the physical first. God made men to feel the final weight of providing physically for the family, church, community, and nation. Chief among these provisions are food, shelter, clothing, and other goods for human flourishing. When God curses the man and woman in Genesis 3 because of their sin, the woman's sphere of childbearing is what brings her multiplied pain (v. 16), while the man's sphere of working the ground is what gives him increased difficulty (vv. 17–19).

The man's call to shoulder the final responsibility of providing food, shelter, clothing, and more for his family does not mean that his wife does not share in such providing. The excellent wife "provides food for her household" (Prov. 31:15), but the man should feel the deepest sense of responsibility for it. Before the food is gone, the clothes are worn, and the house is deteriorating, it is the man who should sense the main pressure to make things happen.

Both the man and his wife will rise to the biblical calling to labor, but the man will uniquely carry the burden to "work with his own hands" to provide for wife and children (Eph. 4:28). It is the man who most deeply feels the scare of the apostolic warning, "If anyone does not provide for his relatives, and especially for members of his household, he has denied the faith and is worse than an unbeliever" (1 Tim. 5:8).

And it's important to note that this call to provision is not about our competency but about God's calling. Likely, women are, on the whole, the more competent gender. But the issue is God-given roles, of who leads in the dance so that the other's beauty will be featured. Together a husband and wife may feel the weight of the warnings against idleness in physical provision in 2 Thess. 3:6–12, but that weight is the husband's to own.

As we'll see in each aspect of provision, mature masculinity both serves women and serves alongside women. Exceptional circumstances exist, like disability, in which a man is unable to take up the role as physical provider as he would otherwise. But typically it is the man's role to provide physically for his wife, and to take initiative, not just be along for the ride, as he and his wife together provide for the children.

Emotional

As husbands and wives pledge together to provide for their children, and the physical aspect falls mainly to the husband, we might think that the emotional falls entirely to the wife. Possibly the single most important thing to say in a chapter on provision is that the husband's and father's call to provide includes but is not limited to the physical. The man who has provided physically for his family has fulfilled only one aspect of the holistic call to provide.

As a husband and father, I love my wife's feminine wiring and remarkable intuition for tracking the emotional pulse of our home. She far surpasses me in her ability to be sensitive to, and dialed in on, the emotional dynamic in our little fellowship. But just because she better monitors and cultivates our emotional well-being doesn't mean I'm off the hook for this aspect of provision. The family inevitably looks to Dad to listen actively, ask good questions, and seek to go beneath behavior and external details to the heart as the one bearing the final responsibility before God.

And most importantly, providing emotionally for the family means that I seek to provide emotionally for my wife, even though she generally is the more emotionally in-tuned person. It is the masculine impulse to seek to grow not just in knowing her heart and pursuing her emotionally, but also in praying myself into being present at home physically *and* emotionally, even when I'm drained from a long day of breadwinning (especially if the husband's vocation is largely intellectual and emotional, and not physical).

Providing emotionally for wife and children means that masculinity is not just about delivering the physical goods, but also about giving good energy—perhaps the hardest energy to give—to gladly assuming sacrificial responsibility, both for what is seen and for what is unseen, the things of the heart. With both wife and children, this means resisting the urge to manage behavior, and instead doing the tough work to discover, and minister to, what's going on beneath the surface.

Intellectual

The intellect can be a polarizing topic. Some seem much too eager to make provision here (to the neglect of other aspects), while others, perhaps hurt by the effects of intellectualism, seem suspicious of the life of the mind. But the Christian must avoid these extremes. The intellect is limited in what it can do, yet so important in what it does. We want "to be renewed in the spirit of [our] minds" (Eph. 4:23) and "be transformed by the renewal of [our] mind" (Rom. 12:2). Among other things, our spiritual growth hinges on the engagement of the mind. Intellectual provision is vital.

One obvious provision in the intellectual realm is education. It is an essential part of growing as a child and flourishing as an adult. Mature masculinity seeks to develop the mind (my own, my wife's, and my children's) and an appetite for lifelong learning—both in the home and outside.

For the wife, outside the home there are opportunities like continuing education and community education and book clubs and friendships with thoughtful individuals—none of which will happen unless the husband has the kids and covers the home while Mom is out engaging and sharpening her mind. Inside the home, where it's easy to default to the details of your day and the minimum communication required to get by with young kids, intellectual provision can mean making an extra effort to share knowledge in a humble way and even research some possible purchase or a new area of interest together.

For the children, outside the home there's schooling and Sunday school and zoos and science museums and field trips, all to be encouraged by a curious dad with energy enough to ask about and engage in—or better, lead or join in himself. At home, Mom and Dad together, with Dad feeling the final burden, should provide for an ongoing acquisition of knowledge that will help the kids become thriving adults. Together, Mom and Dad communicate in and beneath their words the relative importance of homework and academics (neither unimportant nor all-important) and, chiefly, the place of the life of the mind in loving God.

In my four short years as a father, I'm learning that providing emotionally and intellectually for my sons has a lot to do with emotional and intellectual energy. Am I willing, even when I'm tired and spent, to keep digging and, leaning on God, to find the energy of mind and heart to read another (few) book(s), ask another good question (or two), take advantage of a teachable moment, or put in the proactive effort to train the children ahead of time about what to do and what not to do, rather than simply punishing them after they've disobeyed? (For more on discipline, see Andy Naselli's chapter in this volume.)

Nightly, as I pray over my sons at bedtime, with them hearing every word, I ask that God would grow them not only in body and heart, but also in mind. I pray this triad over and over again, and try to evaluate my efforts as a dad in light of this. We want to nourish and cherish our children, not anemically but holistically, in mind and body and heart.

Spiritual

Last, but not least, is spiritual provision, the most difficult and most important. The Christian man will want to work *with* his wife, not against her or apart from her, in providing spiritually for their children. It is a beautiful thing when Mom and Dad, together, sit on the floor with Bible in hand—or the Jesus storybook, for younger children—at eye-level with the kids, their attention focused, hearts ready to marvel, and faces ready to exude joy. For our family, our brief devotions and prayer before bed each night play an important role in our effort to connect spiritually and provide for our sons. (For more on family devotions, see Tony Reinke's chapter in this volume.)

Part of spiritual provision is leading the family in an active relationship with the local church and developing the regular routine of joining together in corporate worship. Prayers of thanks at meals and before scattering for the day are other good opportunities to provide spiritually, along with turning the conversation again and again to Jesus and his gospel as matters "of first importance" in our lives (1 Cor. 15:3). Together with our wives, we will want to teach our children Scripture memorization, gospel songs, and Bible stories culminating in Jesus. Through gentle questions and careful observations, we will want to be in touch with our children's spiritual condition, so that we may know how we can pray for them and how we might supply what is lacking in their faith (1 Thess. 3:10).

In those tender moments each night as I tuck my sons in and turn out the light, I love asking them what was their favorite moment of the day, and the hardest, and then trying to shepherd them spiritually in gentle and simple words on knowing "how to be brought low, and . . . how to abound" (Phil. 4:12–13).

Never forget, though, that the husband, in his masculine calling, not only partners with his wife to shepherd the children spiritually, but also seeks to provide for her. This begins with knowing her as a fellow heir of the grace of life (1 Pet. 3:7) and looking ahead to the day when she "will shine like the sun in the kingdom of [her] Father" (Matt. 13:43). For young husbands, and maybe old ones too, this can be a hard balance to find between spiritual disinterest or neglect, on the one hand, and hovering over her and being over-bearing, on the other. The wise husband will realize that God means for a man and his wife to keep growing in and learning about their oneness for a lifetime. There are times to say less and times to say more. Learn to know her and her needs, not just what's natural to you. As with seeking to care for anyone spiritually, there are times when you may give too much effort out of deeply felt concern, and times when you will give little effort yet see her spread her wings.

In this aspect of provision, we feel most acutely that there is only so much we can do. The final and decisive work is the Holy Spirit's. Which reinforces for us the importance of our vigilance in prayer for our wives and children.

The Great Provider

Though holistic provision for women and children is a greater burden than a man can fully bear, he is not alone. Precisely in the most desperate moments when bearing the masculine role feels most unfair—when we're our most tired, running on fumes, yet need to keep providing in all these aspects—this is when the provision of God tastes the sweetest.

Whether it's physical, emotional, intellectual, or spiritual, God will make sure that you have the provision he has specifically designed for you in the moment. "My God will supply every need of yours according to his riches in glory in Christ Jesus" (Phil. 4:19). It's not always, or usually, the provision we want, but it is always the faultless provision of his perfect plan and lavish love.

While we are called to shoulder the mantel of primary provider humanly speaking, we are not the final provider. God is the Great Provider. It is God who provides us with the Spirit (Gal. 3:5) and God who provides us with strength to serve (1 Pet. 4:11) when our tank is empty. It is God who supplied the sacrifice for Abraham and inspired the name "The Lord will provide" (Gen. 22:14). And it is God who fulfilled, in his perfect timing, what Abraham prophesied, "On the mount of the Lord it shall be provided." As Christian men, we have seen the Provision. And if he "did not spare his own Son but gave him up for us all, how will he not also with him graciously give us all things?" (Rom. 8:32).

The great provision of God for sinners in general, and for you in particular, is the great backdrop that empowers our little efforts at playing the man, whether married or unmarried, shaped by God's good design for us in the masculine calling to provide holistically for those in our care.

This is not an easy calling. But in light of the gospel, it is a happy one.

4

The Feminine Focus

Trillia Newbell

There is no denying that guys and gals are different. Our physical appearance alone says as much, and an important aspect of a woman's femininity includes our physique. But that isn't everything.

God created us in part for childbearing. One of his first means of blessing—and purpose—for men and women is the charge to be fruitful and multiply and to fill the earth and subdue it (Gen. 1:28). From the beginning, we know that children are a blessing and humans have an unparalleled calling.

Unfortunately, because of the fall of man, sin came into the world wreaking havoc on creation, including women and childbearing (Gen. 3:16). Having children does not always go as hoped or planned. There are women who experience miscarriages and infertility. I've had the experience of miscarriage myself. In other cases, some women never get married. Paul refers to singleness (which also means celibacy) as a gift (1 Cor. 7:7). This, among other reasons, is why the physical, while important, should not be made the sole basis of femininity.

As chapter 1 explains, it's not merely physical attributes that make us male and female. Femininity goes much deeper than what we see in the mirror. God created us with roles and instincts that are distinctly feminine, and these are all meant to point to his glory.

He Called It Good

Have you ever tried to bake something, and it turned out a complete disaster? Well, once my friend Emilee and I decided we would attempt to cook a fancy dinner entree called Beef Wellington. It's basically a slab of beef wrapped in a puff pastry. The ingredients included some pricey tenderloin and other specialties that were supposed to form into a beautiful dough that wrapped around the meat. We followed the directions to a tee (so we thought). After two hours of preparing and cooking, we ended up slicing the beef and frying it in a pan. The "pastry" was a doughy mess. It didn't turn out like we hoped. Nothing about our dish resembled the beautiful picture of glistening meat shrouded in a golden-brown pastry. My mouth had watered looking at the picture. Ours wasn't even close.

God has never had that problem. He didn't make one mistake in creating humans male and female. He didn't forget an ingredient. He didn't have to start over or improvise halfway into the process. Why does this matter? Because for us to embrace our femininity, we must first understand that it wasn't an accident. This not only gives us confidence to trust God's design; it should also bring us great joy. The Lord of the universe created us like he intended—and he called it good.

Strength Where It's Needed

The first evidence that God had a unique purpose for men and women is that he made us in his image. This is the most important aspect of our femininity. We were created in the image or likeness of God, reflecting the various characteristics of our Lord (Gen. 1:26; 5:1–2). Something about our femininity is saying something about God. God didn't create Eve on a whim. It wasn't some impulsive move. He knew what he was doing. God had placed Adam in the garden to work the land. Now this wasn't some run-of-the-mill garden. It was the garden of Eden before sin entered the world. Imagine how crystal clear the water would have been, and the lush green grass, and the fruit and sunshine. It was Paradise. And yet, God still determined that Adam needed a helper. Adam was alone, and it was not good.

So God created the female in his image, equal to the man in dignity and yet *immediately* different from the man in role. God created Eve as a helper fit for Adam (Gen. 2:18, 22–23). Remember, this is before sin. God created Eve as a helper, and it was a part of his *perfect* plan. It was good—for the good of Adam and for the good of Eve. Adam needed someone to complement him.

This term "helper" has gotten a bad rap. But it was actually God's solution to an otherwise unsolvable problem. Man needed a helper fit for him. "Helper" in the original Hebrew means the one who supplies strength in the area that is lacking. This isn't a wimpy role! This isn't a wimpy word. We magnify God as we embrace the calling to come alongside our husbands and gladly supply strength where they need it.

My husband and I are different. For starters, he is an introvert; I'm not! But as we continue to grow in our marriage (just over a decade now), I realize that the different and unique way the Lord has designed me—both as a fellow image bearer and as a woman—is precisely where I feel most helpful to him. It helps us grow in grace. For example, obedience to the Great Commission most likely will include having people in your home. I love hosting people and often find myself suggesting invitation plans throughout the year. He enjoys having people over, but his first inclination is not the nurturing intuition that's part of femininity. He'd be content to hang out with just our family, not necessarily put the arms of our family around friends with forethought intention. By reminding him to invite others into our home, I'm helping my husband realize the importance of relationships in making disciples, not to mention the Christian distinctive of hospitality (Rom. 12:13; Heb. 13:2; 1 Pet. 4:9). This is one way I can help—one way I can supply strength where it's needed. This is God's good design.

Moreover, the role and distinction of helper is by no means relegated to a female who is married, though it is most pronounced in marriage. Women in several different environments can actively walk out their feminine characteristic of helper through assisting and encouraging men, including, but not limited to, church, work, and school. It is a joy-filled, God-magnifying role.

The Gentle, Quiet Spirit

The apostle Peter tells us, "But let your adorning be the hidden person of the heart with the imperishable beauty of a gentle and quiet spirit, which in God's sight is very precious" (1 Pet. 3:4). Naturally, my personality doesn't gravitate toward quiet. I am vivacious and charismatic, and slightly opinionated (okay, I'm being nice to myself). But for sure, it's not quiet. Many of you might feel the same way. So what does this verse mean?

In 1 Peter 3:3, Peter begins to contrast the importance of outward appearance to the heart: "Do not let your adorning be external—the braiding of hair and the putting on of gold jewelry, or the clothing you wear." He says instead, "Let your adorning be the hidden person of the heart with the imperishable beauty of a gentle and quiet spirit, which in God's sight is very precious" (v. 4). Women in that day would wear large jewelry and elaborate braids as a signal of wealth. Evidently this would draw attention to these women. It's no wonder that Peter addresses women about our outer appearance.

For centuries we have worried about how we look. The plastic surgery and diet industries alone give ample proof that our concern for outward appearance even today has a strong hold on many women. Truly, nothing is new under the sun. But there is something far greater that should concern us: *our hearts*. Peter is urging Christian women not to be concerned with outward appearance, but instead to focus on their hearts.

There is something quite significant about the heart. We are told in Proverbs 4:23 to keep our heart with all vigilance because "from it flow the springs of life." One commentator says that the heart in Proverbs regularly refers to the center of one's inner life and orientation to God. It is where we think, feel, and look to God. In Ezekiel, we get a glimpse of God's new covenant salvation: "And I will give you a new heart, and a new spirit I will put within you. And I will remove the heart of stone from your flesh and give you a heart of flesh" (Ezek. 36:26). A new heart indicates a new disposition to live for God. He transforms the heart—our innermost being—and our desires begin to align with what God desires for us. This is Peter's concern, and it should be ours.

The Heart Made Strong

To be sure, Peter doesn't say we should not wear braided hair and jewelry. He doesn't want us to be overly focused on it. The heart is the main thing. So when he says to adorn ourselves with a gentle and quiet spirit, he is not referring to our personality. A gentle and quiet spirit is ultimately found in trusting and fearing the Lord.

> Charm is deceitful, and beauty is vain,
> > but a woman who fears the LORD is to be praised.
> > (Prov. 31:30)

When describing a woman who possessed a gentle and quiet spirit, Peter used the example of Sarah, who did not fear anything that was frightening (1 Pet. 3:6). We see this example again found in the valiant woman who laughs at the time to come rather than worrying in fear (Prov. 31:25).

As we grow in our understanding of the goodness and sovereignty of God, our inward being begins to be transformed from anxiety to quietness, from angst to gentleness. This is the heart of a helper—the heart of a woman made strong in God.

The heart is the focus of our femininity—and that's good news because that's where God works. We need him to help us capture the beautiful role of helper, and then fulfill it with joy and gladness. God supplies the grace to be what he calls us to be. We don't have to muster up strength in and of ourselves to be the women to which he's called us. He's the one who starts the good work, and he's the one who finishes it.

5

The Nature of a Woman's Nurture

Gloria Furman

Recently I was doing some reading and chatting with friends on Facebook when my heart was bowled over with the diversity of our experiences.

A couple of expectant parents uploaded a video of themselves slicing into a cake dyed pink inside to announce they were having a girl; a new mom wrote about her frustration with a teething baby's cries and asked for advice; a single woman said that she had just met with some of the teen girls in our youth group; a former coworker posted a photograph of her infant with oxygen tubes in his nose and pleaded, "Please continue to pray. We are still waiting for his transplant. Not out of the woods yet"; a photo of my nephew popped up of him wearing his football uniform; an update appeared linking to a video of pro-life protesters being harassed on a college campus.

Then my son wandered into my bedroom, cheeks flushed and rubbing his sleepy eyes, and said, "I just need you, Mommy." I walked him to the kitchen to get a sip of water, and I noticed some special pictures on our refrigerator. There was a photo of one of our seminary professors and his wife. Though they are of retiring age, they still travel back and forth to the Philippines visiting the churches they planted decades ago. I noticed a Christmas photo of our friends who are standing next to an empty chair that is waiting to be filled with their adopted son still overseas.

As I walked my preschooler back to his room, my mind wandered to a dear friend of mine, as it often does, and I prayed God would comfort her as she continues to grieve her preschooler's death three years ago. In the shadowy bedroom, I looked over to see my daughters sound asleep, limbs adorably flailed across their beds with sheets and toys in disarray—and I felt my heart might explode. We experience so much joy, excitement, and life—and so much pain, anxiety, and death. What finite heart could contain all these things? How do mothers make it? In the midst of all this complexity, what does it mean for a woman to nurture?

The foundation for this topic of women and nurturing is God's Word. We must draw implications for ourselves as God's creation by looking first at God, our Creator. In all our diverse life seasons and experiences, from grandmothers to baby girls in Mumbai to Mobile, the Bible contains timeless, applicable truth about the one for whom we were made. In God's Word, we see God's good design for manhood and womanhood: the triune God made men and women in his image to display his glory. We miss the point of womanhood when our understanding is handcuffed to matters of culturally based stereotypes, mere biology, or procreative abilities. We see in God's Word that womanhood cannot be described apart from talking about God's image, the gospel, and how Jesus Christ is restoring us. Being made as a woman in God's image is surely a *wonder-full* thing.

Motherhood (by which I mean rearing children *and* raising up spiritual children/disciples) is by no means an idol that we serve, but rather an intentional gift God has strategically designed and given us so that we might see his glory and make him shine. This chapter on nurturing is about learning to rejoice in Jesus because motherhood is the work of his hands.

Created in the Image of God

It would seem that something like the image of God would be easily cast into the realm of intangible ideas or lofty thoughts. And though it's profound, it's not overly complicated. God calls mankind his icons—literally *eikon* in the Greek Old Testament. We are his little statues, scattered throughout the world—billions of us. Our existence tells the cosmos and the powers and the principalities just who all of this belongs to. Everything belongs to God.

We should delve into the subject of being made in God's image with humble hearts and big grins on our faces. Do not let this delightful irony get lost on you: we are pondering and commending the beauty of God's design *as creatures* admiring a Creator's work. Our loving Creator has gifted us with the ability to appraise and praise his handiwork. This is astonishing because it implies our potential for relationship with an infinitely holy God. He is set apart from creation as the triune God who exists apart from any creative act or force, and he graciously created finite human beings with the capacity to taste and see his infinite goodness as we apprehend his work and ways. We live embodied in the design that God has so wisely given to us as a gift. This begs the question (in more than one sense): Do we *realize* this?

God created both men and women in his image not for the sake of variety amidst boredom, but with the intended purpose of displaying the glory of his gospel. Eve was not a happenstance addition after Adam. God had in his mind before the foundations of the world to create woman with his divine precision. The complementary designs of man and woman reflect an eternal, immovable reality in heaven—namely, the pre-creation plan for the Son to give his own life to purchase for himself a bride (2 Tim. 1:8–9; Rev. 13:8). There are things that God wants us to see about his gospel as we consider our complementary differences. That means this topic is not just some blasé academic exercise, but our joy in the Lord is at stake. So in all our thoughts about this we need to be informed by the Word of God and remain happily subject to his unparalleled authority to tell us what he has done, is doing, and means to show us about himself.

Then Came the Curse of Sin

When God created Eve, there was no absurd inconsistency in her God-given qualities. She was created in God's image to be Adam's suitable, complementary helper (Gen. 2:18, 20). The woman's equal value with the man, her strength, and her intelligence are not in conflict with her unique role of voluntary submission to her husband's leadership. Together, they are coheirs—Eve's help gladly oriented toward Adam's leadership. But along with the rest of the created order, when Eve fell into sin, her heart turned in on itself. *No one is for your good, not even God, so reach out and take it yourself*—this was the poisonous lie that the serpent hissed into Eve's ears. With a skeptical heart, she stood in judgment over God's word and ate the fruit.

Sin wreaks havoc even now. With heavy hearts, we wonder how our God-given design could be a satisfying gift in this place that is full of fellow sinners who marginalize, oppress, and demoralize women. Women are even turned against other women as we grapple for power in a world locked in a tailspin against God's good plan. This is not how God created us to be.

After God's pronouncement of the curse for their sin, Adam clung to God's promise by faith and again he gave his wife a name. This name was wrought of faith in God's future grace: "The man called his wife's name Eve, because she was the mother of all living" (Gen. 3:20). Adam believed God's promise for a deliverer, and because of God's grace Adam saw through his wife the hope-filled future of humanity. Adam and Eve would continue to be coheirs, ambassadors for God, and dominion takers with differentiated, complementary roles. But how?

Redeemed and Empowered

Even after our first parents sinned in the garden and God justly pronounced a curse, his blessing for mankind could still be heard. God promised a rescuer. Before the creation of the world, God the Son looked forward to this epic pledge of mercy:

> I will put enmity between you and the woman,
> and between your offspring and her offspring;
> he shall bruise your head,
> and you shall bruise his heel. (Gen. 3:15)

Many hopeful and forgetful generations later, a virgin gave birth to a son—the promised serpent-crusher, the seed of the woman, the offspring of Abraham come to rescue all who cling to him by faith.

Jesus overcame God's enemy and rescued God's children by dying on the cross in our place and then rising from the dead. This gospel brings all of our cultural ideals about womanhood into the light. When we hear the promise—or chastisement—that women ought to "have it all," we can experience particular pleasure in the fact that *in Christ* we already have infinitely more than anything this world can offer. In Christ we have every spiritual blessing (Eph. 1:3). We have everything that pertains to life and godliness (2 Pet. 1:3). Jesus makes us new so that we live and work from the resources of his life and work.

Nurturing in the Way of Christ

If womanhood cannot be handcuffed to mere biology, can nurturing be relegated to procreation? Through the gospel we see that fertility and "filling the earth" is something that extends to bearing fruit that will last through discipleship—a privilege and responsibility that every Christian woman gets to enjoy. It is only through the clear glass of the gospel that we can see ourselves in the big picture of God's story. He is seeking worshipers from the nations, and he uses us to gather them.

In the light and power of the gospel, the goal of nurturing is human thriving in the most magnificent capacity possible—that all the nations would see and savor Jesus Christ forever. The call to nurture is the call to lovingly meet the needs of others for Jesus's sake (2 Cor. 4:5).

Cruciform Mothering

Because all motherhood exists for Jesus, all motherhood should be in the way of Jesus. In our obedience to the Great Commission, every woman must look to the Man who is ruling from heaven at the right hand of God. Christ himself puts people in our household and in our sphere of influence, and we rest well knowing that it is the Lord who builds the house. It is God himself who grows the garden, even as we diligently plant and water. By God's grace, we can serve people—husband, child, neighbor, coworker, whomever—because Jesus is sovereign, and he is building his church.

Jesus is the one who redeems people for his own possession. This truth assures us that this work will be effective. We are free from laying claim to any fruit of our mothering labors as if they came from us, and we are free from the fearmongering, workaholic mothering that thinks everything is up to us.

We nurture others with the strength God supplies (1 Pet. 4:10–11). All that energy—the caregiving and discipling and serving and multitasking—is his energy. Everything we lack is found in him. And when we're exhausted, when we feel the dusty earth of the Calvary road, we can remember that it's especially then that the life of Jesus is manifested in us (2 Cor. 4:10). It's then that Jesus gives us more of himself, proving over and over that he is enough, that he is good, that there is more joy in him than in the grain and wine that abound (Ps. 4:7)—or in the kids who never make messes and the dinner that prepares itself and the schedules that operate seamlessly. He is better.

Only Jesus

We need childlike faith to raise up the Lord's children—faith that he is glad to give us. The life of Christ in us is our empowering, equipping, unleashing energy for nurturing others. It is his strength that gives us what we need in order to nurture life in the face of death, even through the million deaths to self we die each day. We need to remember that the little blueberry-sized fruits borne by the Holy Spirit are part and parcel of his kingdom.

There's no way a finite, nurturing heart can hold all these things, but Jesus can, Jesus does, Jesus will.

6

What Is Submission?

Christina Fox

Have you ever played one of those word association games where someone says a word and you say the first thing that comes to mind? Well, what's the first thing you think of when you hear the word *submission*? Is it positive or negative?

In our culture, *submission* is a word that often incites controversy. Articles on the subject explode in cyberspace where lines are drawn in the sand and sides are taken. Sometimes the discussion is productive, and other times words are used like swords in a battle, lashing and slashing at those who stand on the other side.

I believe one of the main reasons for this strong emotive response is what people think of when they hear the word *submission*. For many, the first things that come to mind are words such as *inferior*, *doormat*, or *controlled*. I know that response well. For me, the word *submission* once conjured up negative memories from my childhood of put downs, anger, threats, rejection, and fear.

I viewed the call for wives to submit to their husbands solely through the lens of my personal experiences. In fact, upon leaving home and attending college, I feared men and even the idea of marriage. I vowed to never find myself in a place where I was belittled, pushed around, or threatened. As a result, when I first met my husband-to-be in college, my heart was skittish and resistant. I panicked at the thought of reliving my childhood experience all over again.

In my journey to understand the biblical call of submission in marriage, I've had to travel far. I've had to go back into my past and revisit painful memories. I've had to study God's Word and seek wise counsel. I've had to look back to the cross and then forward to my own marriage. Though it's been a long journey, it's been a good one. Now when I hear the word *submission*, my first thoughts are not fear or threats, but beauty and grace.

Does that sound strange to you? Maybe it does, but stick with me. I hope to explain how biblical submission is beautiful. And in order to understand God's call for wives to submit to their husbands, we need to explore and understand what submission is and what it's not.

Understanding Christian Submission

First, submission in Scripture is not isolated to wives. It's something Christ did when he yielded to the will of the Father to lay down his life for us. "Father, if you are willing, remove this cup from me. Nevertheless, not my will, but yours, be done" (Luke 22:42). Submission is something all Christians are called to do. For example, we are all called to submit to the governing authorities (1 Pet. 2:13–17). Children are to obey their parents (Col. 3:20). And in the body of Christ, believers are to submit to one another (Eph. 5:21).

Then there are a handful of key passages in Scripture where we see the specific call for wives to submit to their husbands: Ephesians 5:21–33, Colossians 3:18–19, Titus 2:5, and 1 Peter 3:1–7. When we read these passages, it's important that we have a proper definition of what the word *submission* means in the context of Christian marriage. John Piper defines submission as "the divine calling of a wife to honor and affirm her husband's leadership and help carry it through according to her gifts. It's the disposition to follow a husband's authority and an inclination to yield to his leadership."[1]

Let's use that definition as we explore further what this call to submission is all about. Ephesians 5 contains a lengthy description of the marriage relationship. Here Paul instructs husbands and wives in their unique roles in marriage:

> Wives, submit to your own husbands, as to the Lord. For the husband is the head of the wife even as Christ is the head of the church, his body, and is himself its Savior. Now as the church submits to Christ, so also wives should submit in everything to their husbands.
>
> Husbands, love your wives, as Christ loved the church and gave himself up for her, that he might sanctify her, having cleansed her by the washing of water with the word, so that he might present the church to himself in splendor, without spot or wrinkle or any such thing, that she might be holy and without blemish. In the same way husbands should love their wives as their own bodies. He who loves his wife loves himself. For no one ever hated his own flesh, but nourishes and cherishes it, just as Christ does the church, because we are members of his body. "Therefore a man shall leave his father and mother and hold fast to his wife, and the two shall become one flesh." This mystery is profound, and I am saying that it refers to Christ and the church. However, let each one of you love his wife as himself, and let the wife see that she respects her husband. (Eph. 5:22–33)

Paul shows us that the purpose of marriage is to reflect the gospel. A husband's call to lead and a wife's call to submit reflect the relationship between Christ and the church. The unique roles that men and women have in marriage serve as a living message of the gospel. The

---

[1] John Piper, "The Beautiful Faith of Fearless Submission," http://www.desiringgod.org/sermons/the -beautiful-faith-of-fearless-submission.

husband models the love that Jesus portrayed in laying down his life for the church. And a wife then models the church's submission to her Bridegroom—the church's trust and respect.

As a wife yields to her husband's leadership in their marriage, she reflects the heart of faith that characterizes Jesus's people. The church follows Jesus as her head and uses her gifts to carry out his mission in this world. Likewise, the wife respects and yields to her husband's leadership as she uses her gifts to complement his good purposes for their marriage and family.

This reflection of the gospel in the marriage relationship is where we begin to see the beauty. The gospel is the glorious story of a King who comes to save his bride from slavery to sin. By his own sacrificial death, he redeems her and restores her back to his kingdom of light. The gospel is a story of love and grace, of humility and sacrifice. And this bride is the church, who is irreversibly united to the King by his unfailing covenant.

Because the gospel of grace is beautiful, the marriage relationship reflecting the gospel is beautiful. As a husband and wife live out their unique callings in marriage, they share in this beauty. They shine a light in this dark world, pointing to Jesus and his grace.

What Submission Is Not

When it comes to the kind of submission that lingers in my memory from childhood, it is not the kind of submission that Paul speaks of in Ephesians 5. Submission is not about forced control. When a man leads his wife, he is leading her to depend on Christ, not on himself. The kind of leadership a husband provides his wife is to encourage her growth in grace and prepare her to be a coheir in the coming kingdom. As Piper and Grudem point out in their book *Fifty Crucial Questions*:

> Any kind of leadership that, in the name of Christlike headship, tends to foster in a wife personal immaturity or spiritual weakness or insecurity through excessive control, picky supervision,

or oppressive domination has missed the point of the analogy in Ephesians 5. Christ does not create that kind of wife.[2]

Submission is also not about belittlement, inferiority, or worthlessness. Scripture teaches that we are to "encourage one another and build one another up" (1 Thess. 5:11). It also says, "Let no corrupting talk come out of your mouths, but only such as is good for building up, as fits the occasion, that it may give grace to those who hear" (Eph. 4:29). And "Husbands, love your wives, and do not be harsh with them" (Col. 3:19).

A wife's submission is also not blind and absolute. Ultimately, Christ is the wife's final authority. As a part of Christ's church, she is *his* bride chiefly. As a wife follows her calling to submit in marriage, she is ultimately submitting to Christ. She also gets her spiritual identity and ultimate strength and meaning through Christ and not through her husband. Though her husband's role is to encourage her and build her up in the faith, Christ is the sole source of her faith.

Marriage and the Gospel

Now that we have looked at what submission is and what it's not, how do we view the challenges we face in marriage? How do we as wives live out this call to submit? And how can the beauty of the gospel shine through in our everyday lives?

The gospel really is central—not only because marriage reflects the gospel to the world, but also because our marriages must rely on the gospel in order to do so.

When we struggle in our God-given roles in marriage, it is the result of sin. When spouses respond in anger toward each other, rather than love, it is because of sin. When one spouse rejects or discounts the other, it is because of sin.

But that is why Christ came.

He came to redeem and restore all that has been broken by sin,

---

[2] John Piper and Wayne Grudem, *50 Crucial Questions: An Overview of Central Concerns about Manhood and Womanhood* (Louisville, KY: CBMW, 1992), 22.

including marriage and all its details. When we fail in our marriages, the only place we can find restoration and healing is through the gospel of grace. We have to return to the cross. Christ's blood is effective to cleanse and heal all our brokenness. Here is where we are compelled to repent, to turn from our sin and to embrace our Savior.

The gospel of grace is beautiful. But we can't do it on our own. Just as our salvation comes by grace, it is through grace that we live out our unique roles in marriage. It is only through the power of Jesus and his gospel at work in our lives that the beauty of submission can blossom in our marriages.

For this to happen, Jesus and his gospel must be our anchor. When my husband and I got married, the congregation sang the hymn "Be Thou My Vision."

> Be Thou my Vision, O Lord of my heart;
> Naught be all else to me, save that Thou art;
> Thou my best Thought, by day or by night,
> Waking or sleeping, Thy presence my light.
>
> Riches I heed not, nor man's empty praise,
> Thou mine Inheritance, now and always:
> Thou and Thou only, first in my heart,
> High King of Heaven, my Treasure Thou art.

This hymn perfectly sums up how Jesus must be first in our lives and first in our marriages. When Christ is our vision, he enables us to submit to our husbands as unto him.

The journey for me has been long. But I've left fear far behind. Now there is trust. And there is beauty, because the gospel is beautiful.

7

Every Day Godward

Tony Reinke

When the apostle Paul said a man must first learn to manage his household before he can manage a church, he must have meant that managing a church is something like managing a household. And that means being a father is something like being a pastor (1 Tim. 3:4–5).

I believe it.

Just like a pastor leading a church, a husband is called to lead his household in many different directions: in pulling his family into greater depths of the gospel, in pushing back the tide of worldliness, in pushing his family up in Godward joy, and in sowing deep seeds of gratitude. Pastoring children is a labor requiring a lot of thoughtful paternal attention. It always has been.

On the heels of Israel's dramatic rescue of Israel from Egypt, Deuteronomy 6 sets forth an ancient (and relevant) model for fathers today:

> Hear, O Israel: The LORD our God, the LORD is one. You shall love the LORD your God with all your heart and with all your soul and with all your might. And these words that I command

you today shall be on your heart. You shall teach them diligently to your children, and shall talk of them when you sit in your house, and when you walk by the way, and when you lie down, and when you rise. You shall bind them as a sign on your hand, and they shall be as frontlets between your eyes. You shall write them on the doorposts of your house and on your gates. (vv. 4–9)

These words are equally applicable for moms, but for the sake of this chapter, I'll focus on how this passage shapes a dad's calling (Eph. 6:4). Although we are separated from Deuteronomy by time and geography and culture, Scripture remains true for every father today. We who are dads are called to the glorious labor of chiseling the words of God deep into the lives of our children, and this labor demands our entire schedule (breakfast and bedtime), all of our situations (activity and inactivity), and all of our locations (our comings and goings). There's never a moment with his family when a father is not on call to love his children by pointing their attention Godward.

Learning as a Dad

As a dad of three kids (twelve, eight, and six), this is what I'm trying to learn myself. As I attempt to serve my family in this Godward direction, here are some of the most valuable lessons I'm learning along the way.

1. DAD LEADS FAMILY DEVOTIONS . . . TO JESUS.

Some dads choose to lead family devotions as a liturgy with a concrete style and format, with a Scripture reading, a short homily, and a concluding hymn. Other dads take a more informal approach. My personality favors the structured approach, but over the years the Holy Spirit has given some of the most impactful devotions to our family when "my plan" has taken sudden turns toward the unexpected.

Take one Monday evening in our house, President's Day 2014.
The family lingered at the table after a meal (and drooled over the
President's Day cherry pie). A few Googled and printed presidential
portraits were scotch-taped to the wall. I opened with a prayer of
thanks for the lineage of American presidents and a prayer for our
current president. As we pushed back the empty plates, I grabbed
my Bible, and we began walking through my carefully planned
devotional. I explained that civil authorities (like presidents) are
God-given blessings for our flourishing. I read Titus 3:1 and 1 Peter
2:13–17. So far, so good.

Next I moved on to explain the goodness of civil punishment
that keeps us safe, and I flipped open to Romans 13:1–7. Here's
where things unraveled a bit. Apparently the Marvel Comics Trans-
lation of the Bible I was reading said, "For rulers are not a terror
to good conduct, but to bad. . . . For he is God's servant for your
good. But if you do wrong, be afraid, for he does not bear the
sword in vain. For he is the servant of God, *an avenger* who carries
out God's wrath on the wrongdoer" (vv. 3–4 ESV). That phrase,
"an avenger," leapt from the page into the ears of my (up until
that point) moderately interested six-year-old son. "The Avengers!"
he said in his own love language (and probably in his Iron Man
pajamas). At this point I could have smiled and nodded and kept
reading, but I felt compelled to stop and go along with the sudden
detour.

There was a connection here. The Avengers are dramatized fic-
tional images of the civil powers God has ordained to preserve
justice and order in society. We walked through each character
briefly—Iron Man, Captain America, The Hulk, and Thor—and
reviewed how each hero helps in the fight for justice. Fascinating
discussions, of course, but I knew I had to turn this unraveling devotion toward Christ. So I asked: "But who is *The* Avenger?" Confused looks. "You know it," I said again. "Who is *The* Avenger?"
Slowly it dawned on them, and the devotion took a sudden turn
to the return of Christ—*The* Avenger—who will return to bring

cosmic peace and order. I had no intention of talking about the return of Christ after President's Day dinner, but that's the way it unfolded in the moment. We ditched the presidents, delayed the pie, and detoured directly to Jesus.

Dads, leading family devotions is our calling, and leading family devotions *to Christ* is our final aim. If I have a liturgy at the dinner table, it looks like this: start by reading the Bible and end with Jesus. What happens in the middle will often unfold in ways unexpected and glorious.

2. DAD MODELS A REAL RELATIONSHIP WITH THE LIVING GOD.

Deuteronomy 6 addresses a father's heart before it addresses the hearts of his kids. And this is by design. God's commands are written first "that *you* [Dad] may fear the LORD your God" and then pass that to "your son and your son's son" (Deut. 6:2). And the point gets restated: "These words that I command you today shall be on *your* heart" (Deut. 6:6). Dad is an *object* of gospel grace from God before he is a *conduit* of gospel grace to his children.

Dads are propped up not as models of moral perfection, but as models of holiness born out of contrition and repentance in the highs and lows of parenting. My kids are watching me, watching to see how I respond to affliction and adversity and to success and victory. God has designed my life to be a legacy I pass on to my children.

3. DAD MODELS JOY IN GOD.

But if my so-called obedience appears to my children as gruff, stern, and stoic, I am lying about God. As a Christian Hedonist, I believe God is most glorified in me when I am most satisfied in him.[1] This is the legacy I want to leave with my children. *Son, God is most glorified in you when you are most satisfied in him. Daughter, God is most glorified in you when you are most satisfied in him.*

---

[1] For the meaning of Christian Hedonism, see John Piper, *Desiring God: Meditations of a Christian Hedonist*, rev. ed. (Colorado Springs: Multnomah, 2011).

This end—this aim—shapes everything about my leadership in the home, and it's not a stretch because if fatherhood echoes pastor-hood, leading my family in joy is central to my success as a dad (2 Cor. 1:24). Dad himself is called to model faith, the all-encompassing embrace of God. In the words of Deuteronomy 6, I am called to love the Lord my God with all my heart and with all my soul and with all my might. More than modeling right moral choices, I must model joy—a mighty, heart-filled, heart-saturated delight in God that spills over into everyday joy.

Dads, the model is incomplete if we model duty with a sour attitude. John Piper, a father of five, says of raising young kids: "Children need to see daddy is happy—happy with God, happy in being with the family, and of course happy in worship at church and happy in devotions at home. If dad is morose, bored, and withdrawn, he is saying, 'That is what it is like to know God.'"[2] And that is simply untrue.

4. DAD REORIENTS HIS FAMILY TO THE METANARRATIVE OF THE GOSPEL (DAILY).

With joy taking such a central role in our homes, the Ten Commandments are not given simply for stoic obedience training. Obedience is designed to flow out from God-initiated deliverance, as Deuteronomy 6 sets forth beautifully in the tender setting of a son who turns his head up to his father:

> When your son asks you in time to come, "What is the meaning of the testimonies and the statutes and the rules that the Lord our God has commanded you?" then you shall say to your son, "We were Pharaoh's slaves in Egypt. And the Lord brought us out of Egypt with a mighty hand. And the Lord showed signs and wonders, great and grievous, against Egypt and against Pharaoh and all his household, before our eyes. And he brought us out from there, that he might bring us in and give us the land

---

[2] John Piper, "Dads, Play with Your Kids," *Ask Pastor John*, podcast, episode 279, February 17, 2014, http://www.desiringgod.org/interviews/dads-play-with-your-kids.

that he swore to give to our fathers. And the LORD commanded us to do all these statutes, to fear the LORD our God, for our good always, that he might preserve us alive, as we are this day." (vv. 20–24)

There's a time for young children to simply learn *yes* from *no* and *obedience* from *disobedience*. Disobedience brings negative consequences; obedience brings positive consequences. By God's grace, this obedience at the training-wheel level can be replaced later by a robust, gospel-centered obedience when our children are old enough to understand the redemptive story of Christ.

And this introduces one of the tensions dads face. We're called to instruct children in two truths simultaneously. First, it's impossible for any sinner to earn God's favor with our best obedience. Such favor with God comes only on the merits of Jesus Christ, applied to us when we embrace him by faith (Phil. 3:2–11). Second, we cannot say we embrace this glorious Jesus if we consistently disobey his commands (John 14:15; 1 John 2:1–6). Both points are essential in our training (and more on the second point in a moment). My point here is simple, but essential. The gospel message is the redemptive supernarrative that covers all of time and history, and the gospel message redefines our very existence. The gospel message is a supernatural story of deliverance that makes Jesus glorious and provides the necessary context for mature obedience. It is our glorious calling, Dads, to reorient our families to Jesus and to this supernarrative every day.

5. DAD TRAINS HIS KIDS IN MORAL VISION.

Out of the reality of Christ's death and resurrection (indicatives), we find the full context and meaning and empowerment for obedience (imperatives). When the moral training wheels come off, the supernarrative of the gospel holds them in balance.

As children grow, they find themselves in more and more situations when Mom and Dad are not around, when immediate consequences for disobedience cannot be meted out. Take school for example. As a family, we have over the years had our three children in a mix of public school, private school, homeschool, and public academy. And while each of these educational options has its particular strengths, every option has its particular weaknesses and temptations for each child. A child tempted to self-exaltation and sinful comparison in a private school may be tempted to laziness in a homeschool setting. A child prone to man pleasing at public school can be just as prone to the pride and elitism of the private school.

In whatever context our children are called to demonstrate maturity in this world, dads are called to envision obedience for them, and this obedience flows out of the gospel. Out of Christ's self-sacrificing love for us, our children are called into the world to show love to fellow students and teachers. We help our kids identify pride and self-seeking as we teach them to pray for the children they meet. By the work of Christ, the Holy Spirit gives us the power for such a radical, selfless morality. The Spirit brings the power necessary for the hope-filled moral vision offered by Dad.

6. DAD MODELS GOD-CENTERED GRATITUDE.

All the blessings our family receives—house, food, sports, movie nights, dinners at home, dinners out, even life and health itself—come from the almighty God who sustains us and provides us with everything we enjoy.

We pray before meals, not only because daily gratitude to God for food is a pattern we find in Scripture (1 Tim. 4:1–5). And that food does not appear on the table like magic. Dinner on the table requires God to call and gift men and women, folks we often don't know. I want my children to know that before we enjoyed bread on our table, there was a farm boy who watched his dad farm, who felt the desire to farm himself, and labored in the soil to raise and harvest wheat. Then that wheat was hauled by a man who was called by God to drive a truck, who delivered the wheat to a bakery where men and women were called and skilled by God to make the bread. Next, another truck brought it to our local store, where a night clerk in the dark hours stacked it on shelves, and then a checkout clerk helped finish the transaction with Mom, and now we have bread on the table for dinner. Why? Because God ordained a string of individuals—men and women—whose lives were meticulously fashioned and woven together into one long line with the aim of providing us our daily bread.

Money doesn't make bread; people make bread. Behind the simple provision is a God who has built a complex chain of sovereignly ordained commerce for the goal that our family would have bread on the table, which we in turn lift up in adoration to the God who somehow orchestrated all these details with the aim of blessing us.

Conclusion

Those are just a few ideas of how leadership in the home gets worked out in my life. And if I sound like an impressive father, it's only because space (and perhaps pride) forbids me from documenting my glowing faults and inconsistencies. Growing as a dad is the fruit of the Spirit's gracious work in making my failures into lessons. And if I have learned anything about being a father, it's that the calling of Deuteronomy 6 is too big for me alone. I need a God, I need a Savior, I need a local church, and I need a wife in the gargantuan work of raising children and leaving them with a glorious legacy that God is most glorified in them when they are most satisfied in him.

8

Discipline for Our Good

Andy Naselli

We tend to hold very strong views about parental discipline, and those views are often rooted in our experience. Perhaps we experienced physical abuse or something we think was close to it, or perhaps we never experienced physical discipline at all. Perhaps we grew up in a church environment that was extremely strict about enforcing guidelines but very weak on applying the gospel to every aspect of parenting. It's important to be aware of how your experience shapes how you view parental discipline. But the most important question to ask is this: What does God's Word teach about parental discipline?[1]

Seven Facts about Discipline from Hebrews 12:4–11

Let's begin by looking at a foundational passage related to parental discipline in the New Testament, Hebrews 12:4–11. The context is that the author is addressing Christians who are suffering. Note the repetition of the word "discipline." The word occurs at least once in every verse except the first one:

---

[1] This condenses Andrew David Naselli, "Discipline: Training Our Children for Their Good," *Journal of Discipleship and Family Ministry* 3, no. 2 (2013): 48–64, available at http://andynaselli.com/how-should-parents-discipline-their-children-is-spanking-wrong.

In your struggle against sin, you have not yet resisted to the point of shedding your blood. And have you completely forgotten this word of encouragement that addresses you as a father addresses his son? It says,

> "My son, do not make light of the Lord's *discipline*,
>   and do not lose heart when he rebukes you,
> because the Lord *disciplines* the one he loves,
>   and he chastens everyone he accepts as his son."
>   [Prov. 3:11–12]

Endure hardship as *discipline*; God is treating you as his children. For what children are not *disciplined* by their father? If you are not *disciplined*—and everyone undergoes *discipline*—then you are not legitimate, not true sons and daughters at all. Moreover, we have all had human fathers who *disciplined* us and we respected them for it. How much more should we submit to the Father of spirits and live! They *disciplined* us for a little while as they thought best; but God *disciplines* us for our good, in order that we may share in his holiness. No *discipline* seems pleasant at the time, but painful. Later on, however, *it* produces a harvest of righteousness and peace for those who have been trained by *it*. (Heb. 12:4–11 NIV)

This passage teaches at least seven facts about discipline:

1. *GOD* DISCIPLINES HIS CHILDREN (VV. 5-7, 10).

This passage distinguishes two categories of people: those who are God's children and those who are not. God's children are his people, that is, believers. And the text says that God disciplines his children.

2. GOD DISCIPLINES *ALL* HIS CHILDREN (VV. 6, 8).

Because discipline is a distinguishing factor between those who are God's children and those who are not, discipline is not one option among others for believers; it's ubiquitous. God disciplines his children, and if you are God's child, he will discipline you.

3. GOD DISCIPLINES *ONLY* HIS CHILDREN (VV. 6–8).

God's discipline demonstrates that he loves you and that you are his child. Discipline is not bad. It's good. It's actually a very bad sign if discipline is absent, because it means that love is absent. God disciplines his children because he loves them.

4. DISCIPLINE IS TRAINING: GOD DISCIPLINES HIS CHILDREN FOR THEIR GOOD (VV. 10–11).

Discipline trains us to be righteous. Discipline is not an end in itself. It *trains* us for a specific end: "for our good, in order that we may share in his holiness" (v. 10).

God's discipline is not sadistic, nor is he lashing out in unrighteous anger, frustration, or revenge. He disciplines with a long-term view for our well-being. His discipline is a means for us to become holy, righteous, and peaceful.

Sometimes people use the term *punishment* synonymously with *discipline*. It is important to distinguish these two concepts since the words can overlap based on how people use them: "Discipline is corrective; it seeks to accomplish a change in the one being disciplined. Punishment is meted out in the simple interests of justice. In bringing up children, parents should be disciplining them. In hanging a murderer, the civil magistrate is not disciplining—he is punishing."[2]

5. DISCIPLINE SEEMS UNPLEASANT AND PAINFUL (V. 11).

If it doesn't seem unpleasant, then it's not discipline. If it doesn't seem painful, then it's not discipline.

I should probably say, "If it doesn't seem unpleasant and painful, then it's not *this kind of* discipline." The Hebrew and Greek words for discipline have a range of meaning. Sometimes they refer merely to teaching, exhorting, or warning and not necessarily to physical discipline or chastening. Teaching, exhorting, and warning are not always unpleasant (though they can be), nor are they always

[2] Douglas Wilson, *Standing on the Promises: A Handbook of Biblical Childrearing* (Moscow, ID: Canon, 1997), 105.

painful (though they can be). But since verse 11 says that discipline *always* seems unpleasant and painful, it must be referring specifically to corrective discipline—the kind that is unpleasant and painful. In the context of human parents and their children, what kind of discipline *always* seems unpleasant and painful? Physical discipline stands out most obviously.

6. GOD'S CHILDREN SHOULD ENDURE GOD'S DISCIPLINE (VV. 5, 7, 9).

This is the burden of the passage in context. We can lose sight of this. In the midst of God's discipline, we may be tempted to "make light of the Lord's discipline" or "lose heart" (v. 5). But the author of Hebrews calls this reminder to endure a "word of encouragement" (v. 5).

7. GOD'S DISCIPLINING HIS CHILDREN COMPARES TO HUMAN PARENTS' DISCIPLINING THEIR CHILDREN (VV. 5, 7-10).

This passage assumes that parents who love their children discipline their children. God himself disciplines his children, so disciplining your children is godly. It is good and right.

So what exactly does it look like when parents discipline their children? Verses 5–6 quote Proverbs 3:11–12, so this Hebrews passage connects us directly to the book of Proverbs. The author of Hebrews assumes that the principles of Proverbs still apply to Christians. The Proverbs are good wisdom for God's people today. So let's trace that thread back to Proverbs to see what it teaches about training our children for their good.

Three Levels of Parental Discipline in the Book of Proverbs

I'm borrowing in this section from Paul Wegner, who memorably systematizes what the book of Proverbs teaches about parental discipline.[3] He argues that there are four levels of discipline in the

---

[3] Paul D. Wegner, "Discipline in the Book of Proverbs: 'To Spank or Not to Spank?,'" *Journal of the Evangelical Theological Society* 48, no. 4 (2005): 715–32, available at http://www.etsjets.org/files /JETS-PDFs/48/48-4/JETS_48-4_715-732.pdf; Paul D. Wegner, Catherine Wegner, and Kimberlee

book of Proverbs. Three are for parents, and the fourth is for the government only:[4]

1. *Teach the guidelines*, explaining appropriate behavior, improper behavior, and negative consequences of disobedience.
2. *Reiterate the guidelines*, issuing appropriate warnings.
3. *Enforce the guidelines*, giving a reprimand with non-corporal punishment or, as needed, with non-abusive corporal punishment.
4. *The government disciplines*, administering more severe punishment for continued disobedience.

We should spend most of our time in level 1 (teach), less time in level 2 (warn), and as little as possible in level 3 (enforce). The severity increases from teaching to warning to enforcing.

For example, here's how this might play out if you are in the grocery store parking lot with your three-year-old:

1. You may *teach* your child by saying, "Please hold Mommy's hand while we walk into the store. This is a parking lot with lots of moving cars, and I want you to stay safe."
2. If you feel your child's little hand tugging out of yours, you may *warn* him or her by saying, "Do you see that car? You could get very hurt if you do not hold onto my hand. Please hold my hand, or if you choose to disobey, [consequence]."
3. If your child pulls his or her hand out of yours and darts through the parking lot, you may *enforce* your guideline by saying, "You did not obey Mommy. You pulled your hand out of mine and ran in the parking lot. So since you chose to disobey, [consequence]."

As time goes by, there should be more teaching and less enforcing. The early years require a shorter distance from level 1 to 3 (i.e., from teaching to enforcing), often getting to level 3 regularly.

Herman, *Wise Parenting: Guidelines from the Book of Proverbs* (Grand Rapids: Discovery House, 2009).
[4] The full table listing passages from the Proverbs can be found in Wegner, Wegner, and Herman, *Wise Parenting*, 32.

Parents may tend to warn, warn, warn, and rarely enforce. They may repeatedly say, "If you do that again, then [threatened consequence]." But these often become vain threats with no real sting.

Level 1. Teach

Parents must clearly explain to their children what they expect from them (cf. Prov. 1:8–9). This takes so many forms, and it happens in every venue of life as parents spend time with their children (cf. Deut. 6:6–9). Parents should

- talk about the gospel and how it applies to all areas of life,
- teach values by modeling for their children what they expect from them,
- state rules to their children,
- explain those rules,
- encourage and affirm their children,
- explain improper behavior in neutral contexts,
- connect sin with its consequences so that children see sin's long-term effects

Level 2. Warn

Warning can save a person from danger (Prov. 2:12a, 16a). God is patient and kind with us, and we should be patient and kind with our children. We need God's wisdom to know when to warn instead of enforce. When we warn, we clearly tell our children what will happen if they do not heed our warning. We warn about both short-term and long-term consequences. Short-term consequences include how we will enforce our guidelines if they break them.

Level 3. Enforce

Wise parents are concerned primarily about their children's hearts, not their external obedience (Prov. 4:23). We don't want children who are *merely* externally compliant like good Pharisees or like the older brother in the parable of the prodigal son.[5] But external disobedience evidences heart problems. It offers opportunities to deal with heart issues. And when children disobey their parents, Mom and Dad need God's wisdom regarding how to enforce their guidelines.

This may involve verbally rebuking our children, revoking privileges, and sometimes physical discipline (e.g., "spanking"). The main idea in Proverbs (especially in four passages that mention "the rod")[6] is that "temporary punishment is better than allowing wickedness or evil to run wild and lead to more serious punishment."[7]

Ten Concluding Applications

Let's conclude with ten wise suggestions:[8]

1. Pray for your children.
2. Evangelize your children.
3. Use multiple levels of discipline.
4. Love your children, and tell them and show them that you love them.
5. Beware of two extremes: (a) not disciplining and (b) over-disciplining.
6. Fathers, take the lead in discipline.
7. Learn how to discipline each of your children most effectively.
8. Distinguish between family rules and the Bible.
9. Be humble about parental discipline; don't be proud and judgmental.
10. Persevere with a long-term view that trusts God's Word.

---

[5] Cf. Timothy Keller, *The Prodigal God: Recovering the Heart of the Christian Faith* (New York: Dutton, 2008).

[6] Prov. 13:24; 22:15; 23:13–14; 29:15.

[7] Wegner, "Discipline in the Book of Proverbs," 723. An increasing number of Christians reject physical discipline (or "spanking") as one of the means of disciplining children. Some argue very passionately that it is wrong for a parent ever to spank his or her child. Prominent books and blogs that argue against spanking raise at least five questions: (1) Does "the rod" represent discipline but exclude *physical* discipline? (2) Is spanking a form of physical and psychological child abuse? (3) Do the proverbs about using the rod refer to young men rather than children? (4) Is spanking an obsolete part of the Mosaic law covenant in the Old Testament? (5) Is spanking antithetical to the gospel? For answers to these questions, see Naselli, "Discipline: Training Our Children for Their Good," 54–58.

[8] For brief explanations of each of these applications, see Naselli, "Discipline: Training Our Children for Their Good," 58–60.

9

Training Our Kids in a Transgender World

Denny Burk

At eleven years old, Josie Romero looks like a normal little pre-pubescent girl. It turns out, however, that not everything is as it seems. Josie was born not as Josie but as Joey, a biological boy. Yet somewhere along the way, he decided that he liked behaving and dressing like a girl. With the support of his parents, Josie has given up any male identity so that he can look and act like a little girl. Having turned eleven, Josie finds himself on the edge of puberty, and he wants to have sex-reassignment surgery to make the change permanent and official. His parents, however, are considering putting him on hormone suppressers to delay puberty so that they can figure out what they want to do next.[1]

I don't pretend to understand all the pathologies that lead a little boy to identify as a little girl. Nevertheless, there is one very telling moment in Josie's story. While looking through some dresses for

---

[1] Tommy Nguyen, "Transgender Children in America Encounter New Crossroads with Medicine," *NBC News*, July 8, 2012, http://insidedateline.nbcnews.com/_news/2012/07/08/12625007-transgender-children-in-america-encounter-new-crossroads-with-medicine.

a photo shoot, Josie comes to his stepfather and says, "Daddy, is this okay? Can I do this?" The stepfather has been uncomfortable with this transition all along, but with this question his resolve completely melts away. Looking back he says, "At that point, all of this became a reality to me. And I no longer had a son. And I had to put all my feelings aside to embrace my daughter."[2]

How do parents get to the point where they are willing to put all their feelings aside to embrace a child's desire to be something other than what God created him or her to be? It is very clear that Josie's stepfather had reservations about accepting his son's desire to be a girl. Nevertheless, he did accept it. Why? The answer is that our society is undergoing a radical transition in its understanding of gender. This transition presents Christians with a challenge. The spirit of the age has redefined gender as a spectrum with no normative connection to one's biological sex. In this way of thinking, people are whatever they think themselves to be. If a girl perceives herself to be a boy, then she is one even if her biology says otherwise. If a boy perceives himself to be a girl, then he is one even if his biology says otherwise. Our society is making gender self-determined, not determined by the biological realities that the Creator has embedded into every cell in our bodies.

The Swing in Consensus

Transgender is the "T" in LGBT. It is also considered the next phase of the gay rights revolution. This is not to say that the revolution is over. It certainly isn't. But it is to say that it is on a path of inevitability. And that is why gay activists are pretty much spiking the football at this point. A survey of the cultural landscape can only lead to the conclusion that their cause has prevailed. Take a look at their primary agenda items over the last twenty years. Practicing homosexuals serving openly in the military? Check. Majority public opinion accepting homosexual behavior? Check. So-called gay

---

[2] Ibid.

marriage legal nationwide? Almost check. There can be no question that Americans have been undergoing a steady change in attitudes about homosexuality.[3]

At some point in the last decade, America went from being a majority "anti-gay marriage" country to a majority "pro-gay marriage" country. The big question is this: How did this massive change come about, and what made it happen so quickly?

In her 2012 book *Victory: The Triumphant Gay Revolution*, Linda Hirshman argues that the gay rights movement began in a weaker position culturally than either the civil rights or women's rights movements that preceded it. Nevertheless, gay activists were able to achieve far more in far less time than either of those groups. Why? Hirshman says, "The movement succeeded, uniquely and in large part because, at the critical moments, its leaders made a moral claim. 'Gay . . . is good.'"[4]

Hirshman is right. The gay rights movement has been making a fundamentally moral claim. It is the triumph of that moral claim that has advanced the wider homosexual agenda as quickly as it has. The public is increasingly seeing the issue as a civil rights issue—the next step in society's march toward greater freedom and equality. To oppose such progress is increasingly seen as backward and irrational. That is why gay rights advocates are not asking for tolerance. They are insisting on endorsement. Because "gay is good," the public space can no longer tolerate those who say it is *not* good. Those who say gay is not good are throwbacks who stand in the way of human rights and social progress.[5]

---

[3] Homosexual relationships have become accepted by more and more Americans over the last decade. According to Gallup polling in 2001, only 40 percent of Americans viewed homosexuality as morally acceptable while 53 percent said that it was morally wrong. By 2012, those numbers had flipped with 53 percent calling it morally acceptable and only 42 percent saying that it is morally wrong. This growing acceptance of homosexuality has coincided with a sea change in American views on so-called gay "marriage." In 2004, only 42 percent of Americans said that so-called same-sex marriage should be legalized. By 2011, support for gay marriage had risen to 53 percent (Lydia Saad, "U.S. Acceptance of Gay/Lesbian Relations Is the New Normal," *Gallup*, May 14, 2012, http://www.gallup.com/poll/154634/Acceptance-Gay-Lesbian-Relations-New-Normal.aspx).

[4] Linda Hirshman, *Victory: The Triumphant Gay Revolution: How a Despised Minority Pushed Back, Beat Death, Found Love, and Changed America for Everyone* (New York: HarperCollins, 2012), xvi.

[5] Denny Burk, *What Is the Meaning of Sex?* (Wheaton, IL: Crossway, 2013), 187–88.

Following the Same Trajectory

To understand the transgender revolution, you have to understand that it is following the exact same trajectory as the so-called gay marriage revolution. One of the key moments in the gay rights revolution was in 1973 when the American Psychiatric Association (APA) removed homosexuality from its list of disorders.[6] Transgender—formerly known as gender identity disorder—was removed last year from the APA's list of disorders.[7] We know this script. LGBT leaders are self-consciously pursuing a redefinition of gender as the next phase of the larger gay rights movement. In a feature-length article for *Newsweek* last fall, E. J. Graff asked and answered this very question, "What's Next?" now that the LGBT cause has triumphed? She writes this:

> So then what? Should the coalition of lesbians, gay men, bisexuals, and transgender people . . . declare victory and disband? Once we can marry the person whom we love, are we done agitating for political change under the rainbow flag? In a word, no. . . . There's a much larger cultural question that deeply deserves our country's attention. It has to do with gender: the way our culture, our politics, and our legal system treats femininity, masculinity, and everything in between.
>
> It may be OK, soon, for a woman to marry a woman and a man to marry a man everywhere in the United States. But it's not even close to being OK for a boy to like Barbies and sparkly pink dresses or to swish when he grows up—or for a girl to be so masculine that people nearly do a double take trying to figure out which sex she fits. It's not OK, yet, for someone apparently born male to grow into womanhood, or for someone who started life considered female to make it clear he's a man.

---

[6] Ronald Bayer, *Homosexuality and American Psychiatry: The Politics of Diagnosis* (Princeton, NJ: Princeton University Press, 1987), 3.

[7] The *Diagnostic and Statistical Manual of Mental Disorders*, 5th ed., has reclassified "Gender Identity Disorder" as "Gender Dysphoria." An information sheet about the new edition of *DSM* explains: "Part of removing stigma is about choosing the right words. Replacing 'disorder' with 'dysphoria' in the diagnostic label is not only more appropriate and consistent with familiar clinical sexology terminology, it also removes the connotation that the patient is 'disordered.'" See "Gender Dysphoria" at http://www.dsm5.org/documents/gender%20dysphoria%20fact%20sheet.pdf.

As for the rest of us, we are still, far more than we understand, herded unnecessarily by our sex—by the stereotypes associated with how a woman or a man should act.

It needn't be this way. And if we as a country make the right legal, cultural, political, and educational decisions in the years to come—if we are willing to listen to, and learn from, those on the gender margins—we can make more room for us all. . . .

What I'm describing—a larger direction in which I believe the LGBT movement is turning next—won't be easy. But it's crucially important. And I have no doubt that, as with the battle for same-sex marriage, breaking the nation out of its gender straitjacket is a fight we can win.[8]

So here is what is coming soon to a pew near you. It is not merely that you will be treated as old-fashioned for holding the line on biblical gender norms. You are going to be facing the same charges of bigotry and discrimination on the transgender issue that Christians have been facing on the gay issue. Breaking the nation out of its so-called "gender straitjacket" will involve making a fundamentally moral claim: "Transgender is good." To oppose that claim will be seen as backward and irrational.

What is the proper response to this rising challenge? A number of things can and should be said, but I want to focus on two obligations that we have as Christians: (1) truth telling and (2) gender discipling.

Truth Telling

We must tell the truth about what the Bible teaches about gender. Among other things, the Bible is clear that there is a normative connection between biological sex and gender identity. The "normative connection" that I am speaking of is not defined by the sociological observation that a certain percentage of the population experiences their own gender in a way that conflicts with their

---

[8] E. J. Graff, "What's Next?," *Newsweek*, September 27, 2013, http://www.newsweek.com/2013/09/27/whats-next-gay-rights-movement-238040.html.

biological sex.[9] That sociological norm knows nothing of the fall and confuses what *is* with what *ought* to be. The norm that we must insist on is the norm that is not normed by any other norm: Scripture.

Last summer, Slate.com published an article about a youth camp for gender nonconforming boys. It's a retreat for prepubescent young men who behave in ways that are feminine. The camp provides a place for parents and children to feel "protected" as these young boys act out in ways that they wouldn't normally in public. In the *Slate* article, there are full-color pictures of young boys wearing dresses, parading down runways, dressing up like princesses, painting their toenails, and putting on makeup—all of it with their smiling parents looking on in approval.

One particular line from the report stands out to me as uniquely revealing. It says, "Although it is unknown if the kids at the camp will eventually identify as gay or transgender—or even if the way gender and sexuality are defined throughout society will evolve—the camp allows the kids to look at themselves in a completely different way."[10] Now think about the utter moral confusion of that statement. According to this author, it's not just these boys' gender that is yet unknown. It's also the very definition of "gender and sexuality" that is still up for grabs. The author admits that the sexual revolutionaries and gender revisionists don't really know where they are trying to lead us. Yet they confidently call us and our children forward to follow them over the cliff.

Parents are already being chastised for not letting their children act out in gender-bending kinds of ways. Why? Because now researchers are saying that gender identity and gender expression are relatively fixed by age five. By eleven or twelve, if a child is still insisting on a transgender identity, that identity is almost certainly going to persist. On this view, trying to undo a transgender identity

---

[9] According to the Williams Institute, about 0.3 percent of the population, or about seven hundred thousand Americans, are transgender (see ibid.).

[10] David Rosenberg, "A Boys' Camp to Redefine Gender," *Slate*, July 15, 2013, http://www.slate .com/blogs/behold/2013/07/15/_you_are_you_looks_at_a_gender_nonconforming_camp_for_boys _photos.html.

is as brutal and damaging to a child as trying to undo sexual orientation, and it results in increased risks of drug and alcohol abuse, depression, and suicide attempts.[11] That is why there are a rising number of reports about parents who are letting gender-confused children undergo hormone therapy to delay puberty indefinitely until a decision can be made about gender reassignment surgery.[12] Why? Because the moral claim that "transgender is good" is so intense that it is permissible to surgically alter a child's body to match his sense of self, but it is bigoted to try and change his sense of self to match his body.[13] Yet we have to ask the obvious question: If it is wrong to attempt to change a child's gender identity (because it is fixed, and meddling with it is harmful), then why is it morally acceptable to alter something as fixed as a biological body of a minor?[14] The moral inconsistency here is plain.

This is exactly where the Christian vision of humanity has so much to offer us. The Bible puts solid ground beneath our feet so that we don't have to guess at what it means to be male and female, and so that parents don't have to sow even more confusion into their child's bewilderment. The spirit of the age tells us that raising a little boy to be a little boy can be cruel and abusive if that little boy wishes to behave like a girl. *Gender is a choose-your-own-adventure story, and the parent's job is to get out of the way and let it happen.*

The Christian vision is so very different from this and so very freeing and affirming of what we were really meant to be before God. In the biblical view, every single person is created in the image of God. God did not make us into undifferentiated genderless automatons. On the contrary, he made us male and female (Gen.

---

[11] Graff, "What's Next?"

[12] Denny Burk, "The Little Boy Who Wanted to Be a Girl," *Denny Burk* (blog), http://www.dennyburk.com/the-little-boy-who-wanted-to-be-a-girl.

[13] See chapter 1, "[Transgender] individuals grant [their existential perspective] the ultimate authority and attempt to manipulate the other perspectives [of biology and societal witness] through the use of hormones and surgical procedures. Ironically, the goal of becoming transgender is to have all three perspectives saying the same thing, even if by inauthentic, superficial means" (pp. 29–30).

[14] I got this question from James M. Kushiner, "Why Is Reparative Therapy Illegal for Boys but Gender Surgery for Girls Not?," *Mere Comments*, August 30, 2013, http://touchstonemag.com/merecomments/2013/08/reparative-therapy-illegal-boys-gender-surgery-girls.

1:26–27), and that fundamental biological distinction defines us. Gender norms, therefore, have their roots in God's good creation and are revealed in nature and Scripture. The task of parenting requires understanding those norms and inculcating them into our children—even those children who have deep conflicts about their "gender identity." This is a truth-telling discipline that rests on the Bible's normative connection between biological sex and gender identity. But this assumes that we know what the Bible teaches about manhood and womanhood.

And that brings us to our second obligation. We are not only to be truth telling but also to be gender discipling.

Gender Discipling

If it is true that God reveals gender norms according to biological sex, then making disciples and raising children necessarily involves teaching them to live within biblical norms of manhood and womanhood. Christian, this necessarily puts us in a countercultural posture. But it also raises a question for us. What are we to do with culturally encoded definitions of gender? Does manhood equal machismo? Must all men like sports, the outdoors, grunting, and leaving the seat up? Do such stereotypes equal masculinity or is there something else? Does womanhood equal opinionless passivity? Must all women be focused on their appearance, shopping, and cute shoes? Or is there more?

The response to these questions from some has been to rebuke those who equate cultural norms with biblical norms. "How dare you say that a man cannot wear skinny jeans! There is no biblical prohibition on skinny jeans. That's just your cultural prejudice coming out." To which someone else responds: "So is it okay for a man to wear a dress and lipstick? Is that just a cultural prejudice coming out too?" In other words, the transgender challenge forces us to define the relationship between biblical gender identity and culturally encoded expressions of that identity. The transgender challenge, however, does not allow us to declare culturally encoded gender expressions as matters of indifference. See, for example, as mentioned in chapter 1, the connection that Paul makes between God-given gender roles and head coverings in 1 Corinthians 11.[15]

This means that we will be called upon to bring our consciences into line with biblical gender norms. No, the essence of manhood isn't culturally defined. The biblical norms are what they have always been: the fruit of the Spirit expressed in sacrificial servant leadership, protection, and provision. Discipling men and raising boys will mean shaping men to define their masculinity by these ideals. Likewise, the essence of womanhood must not be culturally defined. It must be marked by the fruit of the Spirit expressed in the biblical norms of helping, subduing creation, and a primary responsibility to home and childrearing.

Conclusion

I serve as one of the pastors in my local church. As a church, we have been praying for one of our members—a young college coed who recently befriended a transgender student in one of her classes. In many ways, she was intimidated and bewildered at the beginning about how to relate to this transgender student. She wondered, "Do I call him by his real name or the female name that he has assumed? Do I refer to him with masculine pronouns or feminine ones? Can I be a faithful witness if I acknowledge in my speech his projected feminine identity?" These were all questions she had as she tried to reach out to this student. But recently she told me that the biggest prayer need she feels is this: "How do I love this person, but still be truthful about where I stand?" The question she's asking is the same one that all of us are facing: How do we speak the truth in love when so many do not regard the truth as loving?

---

[15] This is precisely what Paul is addressing in his comments on head coverings in 1 Corinthians 11. Much debate has focused on the nature of the head covering that Paul refers to. Was it a shawl of some sort? Or perhaps wearing the hair up? Or some other kind of covering? Perhaps none of the above? In spite of continuing disputes on that point, we can say that culturally encoded definitions of masculinity and femininity are in play here. E.g., Richard B. Hays, *First Corinthians*, Interpretation (Louisville, KY: John Knox, 1997), 191: "Our dress and outward appearance should appropriately reflect our gender identity."

Thank God that we do not have to choose between telling the truth and loving our neighbor. Indeed, love always rejoices in the truth (1 Cor. 13:6). So we love our neighbors best when we give them the truth. The truth begins with the gospel of Jesus Christ and eventually communicates the Bible's larger vision of gender and sexuality. And it is this vision that we must be pursuing. The transgender challenge is a symptom of what happens when a society has lost its way. It also shows us how much the church needs to be a counterculture bearing witness to the glory of gender differences that God has made. We bear witness not to constrain and condemn, but to show the world that the happiest and most joyful way to live is in line with the Creator's design. God has made us all in his image as male and female (Gen. 1:27). And there is great glory and happiness in embracing his purposes for us. God's glory and our happiness are not at odds when it comes to gender. They are intimate friends.

Parents, love your children by leading and modeling for them God's design for them as male and female. This will redound to their great joy, to the joy of others, and for the glory of God.

10

Good News for the Not-Yet-Married

Marshall Segal

There is a new epidemic in our nation, and even in our churches. It's called the not-yet-married life.

Sure, there have always been unmarried people longing for marriage, but the statistics suggest that this group is growing at an unprecedented rate in American history. In 1956, according to the United States Census Bureau, the average age at which a man was married for the first time was 22.5. For women, it was 20.1. Those numbers climbed steadily for years, then more dramatically beginning in the 1970s. As of 2014, the numbers reached the ages of 29.0 for men and 26.6 for women.

Now, singleness itself is not necessarily something to be remedied for the Christian. After all, Paul sings the praise of singleness when he lists the spiritual benefits of being spouse-free in 1 Corinthians 7. The single life can be (relatively) free from relational anxieties (v. 32) and worldly distractions (v. 33), and wide open for worship, devotion, and ministry (v. 35). Paul concludes, Skip the ceremony, literally, and enjoy "your undivided devotion to the Lord."

So this relatively new demographic of not-yet-married men and women in their mid to late twenties has the real potential to be a potent vehicle for the worship of God and the spread of his gospel. This means we don't necessarily need to sound an alarm as our young people get married later and later. Without a doubt, within this trend there will be complacencies to confront and immaturities to manage and even evils to fight. But ultimately it might merely be God's means of freeing up a generation to take their devotion to Christ deeper and further into the broken world in which we live.

Will I Be Single Forever?

The hope for a freshly mobilized unmarried demographic is real, and singleness really can and should be celebrated when God uses it to win worship and joy and life in himself. But one of the implications of these statistics is that a growing number of people in the church desire marriage—even feel *called* to marriage—and yet they have to wait longer to experience it. As Christians, we believe the vast majority of people are wired by God to receive and express love in the context of a covenant, so we shouldn't be surprised that this growing phenomenon is hard on lots of our young men and women.

Maybe it's an increasing consumerism in dating and marriage, where people are pickier because there are more choices (especially through mediums like online dating). Maybe it's the lengthening of adolescence, in which twentysomethings less and less feel the need to grow up and take on responsibilities of starting a family, owning a home, and so forth. Maybe it's the success of women in the workplace, creating more vocational opportunities for females that could delay the pursuit of a partner and family. Whatever the root(s), it's a reality. If you have single people in your church, you very likely have unhappily single people in your church, and that crowd is not getting any smaller.

The scary question for us in the waiting is, Will I be single forever? Would God really withhold the good gifts of love and marriage and intimacy and children from me?

None Single, No Not One

First, we need to anchor our feelings of loneliness and longing in the gospel. If we are in Christ, there's really nothing single about us. We all know there are intimacies that are—and should be—unique to marriage, but those that matter most really can be experienced in the bride of Christ, his church. A husband or wife may help and provide for you in ways others can't, but a true, Spirit-filled, persistent, and present brother or sister in faith can care for you in remarkable ways.

These relationships, born and built in the gospel, offer you all kinds of love and intimacy. In this love for one another in the household of faith, we find affection (Rom. 12:10), comfort (2 Cor. 13:11), relief (Gal. 6:2), kindness (Eph. 4:32), encouragement (Eph. 5:19), honesty/truth (Col. 3:9), forgiveness (Col. 3:13), guidance and correction (Col. 3:16), protection (Heb. 3:13), prayer (James 5:16), and hospitality (1 Pet. 4:9). In waiting for our wedding day, we really don't have to wait for any of these things. God has already provided them for us through one another in the living, gifted body of the local church. If we are part of *this* family, we are *not* single. We might not be married, but we are planted in an everlasting community and therefore surrounded with lasting love, affection, security, and a thousand other relational benefits.

These kinds of relationships don't happen by accident. You won't experience the comforts of Christian friendship without working for them. Before anyone can serve you, you need to put yourself in the path of his or her love. Join a small group, or start one. Find a couple of men (for men) or women (for women) to share life and prayer with regularly. Serve with a ministry through your church or in the local community, and be intentional about getting to know the people working alongside you. Don't expect helpful, meaningful relationships to just happen to you. It will require a lot of initiative from you, but we can't live in the fullness of the joy, love, and life God promises without this kind of community, *especially* when we're not married.

Paradise and the Purpose of Marriage

No one in Christ is single, and no one in heaven is married. Jesus makes it abundantly clear that no one stays married or gets married in the age to come (Matt. 22:30; Mark 12:25; Luke 20:34). Marriage has no purpose in the coming paradise. In the happiest place in history, there will be no weddings, no matrimony, no sex.

That's a wild way for God to design this all to work out. If marriage between a man and a woman is such a beautiful, pivotal, necessary relationship and picture for so many in this life, why would it be left out of eternity? It's because its purpose and meaning are only needed here and now. When the new creation is consummated, the picture to which marriage points will be realized. In light of this destination, marriage now is a temporary experience meant to envision a far greater relationship and reality to come, when we are with Christ in his presence.

If we are married in this life, it will be for a brief moment, and we won't regret that brevity ten thousand years from now. We really won't. I won't say, "I really wish I had married," much less, "I really wish I had been married for five or ten more years." Saying that would be absurd when those years seem like seconds compared with all the gloriously, thoroughly happy time we have when the marriage ends at death. We need to think about that as we weigh the intensity of our desperation to have it now. We need to ask whether we have made marriage a qualification for a happy and meaningful life. Am I undone and miserable by the prospect of never being married? Do I think of myself as incomplete or insignificant as an unmarried believer? These questions might reveal red flags warning us that marriage has become an idol. Ultimately, we will be single forever, and it will be gloriously good. Marriage truly is a small and short thing compared with all we have in Christ forever. And I'm writing that as a currently not-yet-married man longing for the temporary this-life experience.

The Nitty-Gritty of the Not-Yet-Married Life

While not an exhaustive or comprehensive guide to navigating the crazy waters of the not-yet-married life, here are a few practical points for men and women. What I am assuming with these points is that there are those in the church who are unmarried, but feel a godly desire to be married.

Not-Yet-Married Men

Single men in the church must learn what it means to be godly single men—to live out biblical manhood in the way you treat any woman who is not your spouse, especially anyone you might be interested in making your spouse one day.

1. TREASURE AND TREAT *EVERY* BELIEVING WOMAN AS A SISTER.

First Timothy 5:1–2 calls us to treat older men in the church as fathers, older women as mothers, younger men as brothers, and younger women as sisters. Aside from the sarcasm, irritation, and sibling rivalry, how do we treat our sisters? Paul is assuming that we feel a natural and intense compulsion to respect and protect the precious daughters of our parents and that we would demand others do the same. In a world filled with the exploitation of women, men of God must make it their mission to preserve, promote, and protect the beauty, integrity, and vitality of our sisters. It will honor and uphold God's purpose for his daughters, and it will set us apart as a testimony to whole societies enslaved to sexual domination and manipulation.

When it comes to pursuing a young woman as a potential spouse, the sibling simile is not necessarily the *only* paradigm, but it should be the prevailing one. It's absolutely right to feel uncomfortable if we have romantic feelings for a biological sister, but we ought to feel just as uncomfortable when we treat sisters in Christ without a real, vigilant regard for their spiritual and emotional protection.

2. ESTABLISH PATTERNS IN FRIENDSHIP AND ROMANCE THAT CONFOUND THE WORLD.

In America today, treating women as our sisters in Christ will mean establishing boundaries in our friendships with women that communicate our desires and intentions clearly and maintain purity of body and heart. It will mean being willing to come across as old-fashioned and even overly cautious or protective. Because of what is at stake, though, and because of the sexual fallenness of our society, I pray that our Christian dating would be dramatically, noticeably different, even "silly" in the eyes of the world around us. If there's nothing about the way we pursue marriage that confounds a twenty-first-century unbeliever, we're very likely not doing it right.

Be especially careful what your behavior communicates to female friends. In our oversexualized culture, flirtation has become a native tongue, especially in our high schools and colleges. Fight the temptation to try and win affection or admiration through cavalier, empty, and suggestive lines and attention. Instead of always trying to create curiosity, be known for pure motives and unmistakable clarity.

3. PRIZE CLARITY AND NOT INTIMACY IN YOUR DATING RELATIONSHIPS.

Manhood in dating means many things, but whatever it is, it should be marked by a purposeful and selfless pursuit of clarity, and *not* the reckless intimacy common to so much dating today. The greatest danger of dating is giving parts of our hearts and lives to someone to whom we're not married. Dating can be fun, but we should never date simply for fun. It is a significant risk, and many, many men and women have deep and lasting wounds from relationships because a couple enjoyed emotional or physical closeness without a lasting, durable commitment. Cheap intimacy feels real for the moment, but you get what you pay for.

While the great prize in *marriage* is Christ-centered intimacy, the great prize in *dating* is Christ-centered clarity. Intimacy is safest in the context of marriage, and marriage is safest in the context of clarity. The purpose of our dating is to determine whether the two of us should get married, so we should focus our effort and attention there. In our pursuit of clarity, we will undoubtedly develop levels of intimacy—it's an unavoidable part of getting to know and love someone—but we ought not do so too quickly or too naively. Be intentional and outspoken to one another so that, as Christians, you consciously regard intimacy before marriage as dangerous, but clarity as unbelievably precious.

Not-Yet-Married Women

In the same way, single women in the church have to learn what it means to be godly single women—to live out biblical womanhood in the situations and decisions unique to females in the church today. This has implications for how a single woman relates to a man.

1. HE REALLY OUGHT TO BE A TRUSTED FRIEND BEFORE HE'S A BOYFRIEND.

Statistics and experience tell us that women and men by nature crave different things—or at least similar things in different proportion—when it comes to marriage, sex, and dating. Women, it seems, are made to desire affection and protection in greater measures. The Bible teaches that women are equally valuable, useful, and vital in God's eyes, but they're also vulnerable (1 Pet. 3:7). So in God's design, men are to bring strength, stability, and provision to women in marriage.

There are experiences in dating that mimic protection while actually endangering a woman. A guy may offer you things that feel safe, warm, and reliable, but the not-yet-married-to-you him can't really give you the kind of safety and security for which your soul longs. When everything feels fun and dreamy, be willing to ask the harder, less romantic questions. Do I trust him? Am I noticing patterns of pride or selfishness? What am I seeing in his spiritual life and disciplines? Do I feel pressured to do things that feel inappropriate? Is he involved in some kind of serious and regular accountability with other Christian men? Before you trust him with more of your heart in a dating relationship, you need to be determining whether he's the kind of trustworthy *friend* who will care for and protect you in your pursuit of clarity about marriage.

2. DON'T LOSE TOUCH WITH DAD.

Sadly, dads are less and less involved in their daughter's dating. It actually makes for a very dangerous situation because God really means for spiritual headship and leadership to be a seamless hand-off, not a disjointed affair that leaves the young woman spiritually and emotionally uncovered from age fifteen until her wedding day. We've relegated dads to a last-minute interview before engagement, when God meant for them to be active, available agents of wisdom and safekeeping. And I don't mean policemen. Foolish dads relish the gun-bearing, tough-guy role. The wise dads relish the opportunity to develop a real, intentional, grace-and-truth relationship with the man who might be tasked with caring for his daughter for the rest of her life.

Now, a lot of young women don't have fathers who love Jesus or want to be involved in their daughters' love life. Some grieve the loss of their fathers. It's tragic, and our preaching, discipleship, and counseling ought to be addressing this need all the time. A godly daughter trying to find a godly husband needs a father to help shepherd her heart and thinking. Fortunately, God very often provides fathers when there isn't a father. It might be another family member or a trustworthy friend of the family or a faithful man in your church. Women, don't skip this step in the process. Make it a qualification for dating that the man get to know an older godly man who you know loves you, preferably your father.

3. ONLY SPIRITUALLY MATURE AND INDEPENDENT WOMEN SUBMIT IN HEALTHY WAYS.

In a world increasingly filled with opportunities for women in the workplace and everywhere else, there can be great confusion about how complementarity really applies. It often is caricatured as the subjugation of women, perpetuating the notion of their weaker position and worth in society. This, in God's eyes, really could not be further from the truth. God intends Spirit-filled, gifted women to grow and flourish in the family, the church, and the world around them. By all means, grow in your relationship with Christ and develop all the gifts God has given you. God-glorifying, world-changing marriages need strong, godly, independent men *and* women.

What does this mean? This means a woman needs to be just as committed as anyone to developing spiritual, emotional, and social maturity that serves her future family—husband and children—as well as her current family in the local church. If a woman is to help and submit in an effective and godly way, she needs to be continually growing in her own affections, critical thinking, decision making, knowledge of God and his Word, humble obedience, ability to communicate, and other areas. Complementarity is not a damsel-in-distress model for men and women. It is the employment of gifted, God-empowered people in different, but indispensible roles. Don't look to a husband to be a hero for the helpless. He needs a helper, partner, and wife who brings passion, wisdom, and strength to their marriage and ministry together.

The End of Your Single Life

If you live the not-yet-married life in and with Christ, it can be a remarkable life. As limited, discouraged, and incomplete as you may feel at times, God *has* loved you, and he *has* given you everything you need to live a full, meaningful, and connected life even now. If the Lord brings a partner, marriage will be a new and unique opportunity to make much of God before the watching world around you. But you don't need to wait until that day to make a difference.

The Bible says that our nonmarital friendships and relationships really are filled with power and purpose.

First, *the world will see the supremacy of Christ in our practical, visible love for one another.* After kneeling down to the ground to wash the disciples' feet, Jesus said, "By *this* all people will know that you are my disciples, if you have love for one another" (John 13:35). If you want Jesus to look important, powerful, attractive, and worthy in your life, love your friends well. Lay down your life for them the way Jesus laid down his for you. Joyful, selfless sacrifice stands out in this world, and it's one of the most dramatic, most persuasive ways to commend Christ and his good news to others.

Second, *our love for one another echoes the love of Christ, holds out hope to others, and climaxes in more and more glory for our God.*

> May the God of endurance and encouragement grant you to live in such harmony with one another, in accord with Christ Jesus, that together you may with one voice glorify the God and Father of our Lord Jesus Christ. Therefore welcome one another as Christ has welcomed you, for the glory of God. (Rom. 15:5–7)

The harmony we have with one another is the instrument through which we sing the glory of God. The way we welcome one another declares the matchless beauty, unrivaled power, and flawless holiness of our God. All of that is wrapped up in the relationships we start and build with believers around us.

Third, *this love—not marital love—fulfills the law of Christ, living out the character and purposes of God.* "Bear one another's burdens, and so fulfill the law of Christ" (Gal. 6:2). What the law was aiming for, love among believers accomplishes. God set forth a full, powerful, even intimidating picture of his character and holiness when he gave his people the law. When Christ comes, he saves us, writes the law on our hearts, and fulfills the law's purpose in our love for one another. This is speaking not of marital love primarily, but of *all* love between brothers and sisters in faith.

As we wait upon God's will for marriage in our lives, we need new eyes from him to see the depth and significance of what we enjoy within the church. We cannot afford to underestimate or underinvest in such relationships. Our witness to Christ, our message of hope, and the glory of God are at stake with these roommates, coworkers, girlfriends or boyfriends, and friends. Let's pray and dream together about how to make this not-yet-married life count. Let's make our pursuit of marriage another loud-and-clear statement of our fidelity to Christ and our desire to further God's work in our world.

11

Purity We Can Count On

Grant and GraceAnna Castleberry

When Grant and I started dating, my dad, who is a pastor in South Carolina, told both of us (separately) that he had two rules for us before we were married: "You can hold hands after you get engaged, and you can kiss after you say your vows." These "two rules" seemed a bit extreme to me, but later, during our premarital counseling, my dad explained to both of us that his rules were there not to inhibit our joy, but to help us pursue Christ and our joy more fully by walking according to his Spirit, not according to the flesh (Eph. 5:18). Looking back, I'm thankful that he helped us avoid temptation and keep our eyes on Jesus.

One of the misconceptions about sexual purity that both of us have seen and heard is that it's merely a set of rules before marriage. This assumes that lust will end when you get married, which is untrue. It also gives the impression that purity is merely a matter of externals versus an issue of the heart. Yet it *is* about the heart, and the reality is, we are all impure. True purity is possible only in Jesus Christ and the good news of his death and resurrection. Apart from him, our self-strengthened attempts to be pure amount to nothing more than filthy rags. Moreover, purity is not the end in itself, but Jesus is. Purity is actually a continual journey of being conformed into his holy image. That's why the apostle Peter's exhortation to be "holy" is not merely abstract, but a call to "be holy" because God is "holy" (1 Pet. 1:16). The radical nature of the gospel is this: those whom the world considers impure and unclean can be infinitely pure and clean in Jesus Christ.

The Impure Made Pure

When I (Grant) was deployed on a Marine Expeditionary Unit, one of our port calls was at Pattaya Beach, Thailand, a city known for its sex tourism, prostitution, and transsexual cabaret shows. I spent most of my time during the port call catching up on sleep at a secluded hotel, reading, and talking with my wife on the phone. But on one night, I worked a shift of "Shore Patrol" duty. As part of this duty, I had to walk up and down "Walking Street," the main street where the brothels and shows are all located. As I traveled the street with the other men on patrol, we could not walk ten feet without being beckoned by young fifteen- to twenty-year-old girls. They were everywhere. And I knew, from what I had heard, that most of them would work the streets and send their money back to their extremely poor families. It was eye-opening and heartbreaking, all at the same time. I was disgusted by the "sex tourists" and the wealthy Westerners I saw going in and out of these establishments, and I was heartbroken for these girls, who found themselves living the lowliest type of life, with seemingly no hope.

Interestingly enough, also in Thailand, there are over thirty-three thousand active Buddhist temples. The ordained Buddhist monks and nuns who run these temples have all pledged to live a life of celibacy, engaging in absolutely no sexual activity. Many look upon such abstinence as very "pious" and "spiritual."

But the amazing reality of the gospel, incomprehensible to the world, is that one prostitute who repents of her sin and clings to Jesus is more holy and pure than the most devout Buddhist monk.

How can this be? How could someone who has lived as a prostitute be pure, while a celibate monk is seen by God as impure and unrighteous?

All Have Fallen

First, Christianity views purity differently from the way the world views it. It is not just our actions that are judged, but also our thoughts, our intentions, our desires. Jesus said in Matthew 5:27–28, "You have heard that it was said, 'You shall not commit adultery.' But I say to you that everyone who looks at a woman with lustful intent has already committed adultery with her in his heart." Jesus's point is that God is not impressed if we merely abstain from fornication and adultery. He demands that our hearts be so pure, we refuse to look upon someone with any hint of sexual immorality.

Paul hammers the same point in Ephesians 5:3 when he connects covetousness to sexual immorality: "But sexual immorality and all impurity or covetousness must not even be named among you, as is proper among saints." Then, as if the bar were not high enough, Paul states negatively, "Whatever does not proceed from faith is sin" (Rom. 14:23), and also positively, "Whether you eat or drink, or whatever you do, do all to the glory of God" (1 Cor. 10:31). In other words, God's standard for righteousness is so high that if we perform any action outside of faith in his beloved Son and for his cherished glory, it is considered sinful and impure.

When we are measured by these standards, no one can be considered pure. No one. We have all fallen short of God's standard of purity in every possible way (Rom. 3:23).

The One Pure Man

But the wonderful message of the gospel is that Jesus Christ took on human flesh and lived a perfect life for us. He never looked at a woman with lust in his heart. He never stole an illicit glance. He never "let his guard down" and "caved in." He was himself purity incarnate. He took on our sinful humanity, without any guilt, and lived the life of purity we were created to live but couldn't. Therefore he was qualified to pay the sin debt that we owed. He cleansed us of sin, purifying us before God the Father (Heb. 1:3).

That's what Christ did for his church—he loved her "and gave himself up for her" (Eph. 5:25) so that she may be "cleanse[d] from all unrighteousness" (1 John 1:9). When we place our trust in Christ, the purification Christ purchased for us is applied to us through faith.

But purification is not the only thing we receive. Paul also says that in faith, we receive the righteousness of Christ (2 Cor. 5:21)! As Sinclair Ferguson says, "In Christ a 'wonderful exchange' took place. He became what he was not, a condemned criminal, in order that we might become what we are not, men declared righteous and justified in the sight of God."[1]

His Mercy in Our Purity

This is where Paul begins his exhortation to us to be pure. He implores us to reflect on who God has already made us to be in Christ. "I appeal to you therefore, brothers, *by the mercies of God*, to present your bodies as a living sacrifice, holy and acceptable to God, which is your spiritual worship" (Rom. 12:1).

Paul in Romans is exhorting us as those whose lives have been changed by grace to act as those whom God has created by his mercy, those who have been justified by faith (3:24), reconciled in hope (5:11), raised with Christ (6:5), indwelt by the Spirit (8:11), adopted as God's children (8:15), called to his forever fellowship (8:28), foreknown before the world (8:28–29), predestined to be like Christ (8:29), loved without inhibition (8:35), chosen as surely as God is faithful (9:23–26), and declared righteous in his power (10:4). It is with these amazing and life-changing acts of mercy in

---

[1] Sinclair B. Ferguson, *The Christian Life: A Doctrinal Introduction* (Edinburgh: Banner of Truth, 1989), 87.

mind that Paul exhorts us to be living sacrifices and a holy people—because that is who we already are in Christ.

Forward through the Cross

So how do we live as pure people, since that is who Christians are in Christ? Paul continues in Romans 12 by exhorting us not to be conformed to the world, but rather to be transformed by having our minds renewed. This draws out several important implications for our purity.

Negatively speaking, if we surround ourselves and fill our minds with impure things, these will often wreak havoc. So, even though we are believers in Christ—pure in Christ positionally—we can still think impure thoughts, which often lead to sinful actions. Therefore, we should be intentional about avoiding temptations to sin by identifying what tempts us, and we should pray to God that he would not lead us into those temptations (Matt. 6:13). Upon this prayer, resting in God's faithfulness, we should then strive to actively avoid those temptations. Paul goes on to say in Romans 13:14, "But put on the Lord Jesus Christ, and make no provision for the flesh, to gratify its desires." This means that believers should be marked by an aggressive intentionality that identifies weak spots and temptations and strives to avoid those pitfalls.

Positively, Paul also says to put on Christ (Rom. 13:14), to seek righteousness and the things of God (2 Tim. 2:22), and to be transformed by the renewing of our minds (Rom. 12:2). The Holy Spirit renews our minds when we avail ourselves of his means of grace. It's here where we are filled with the Spirit to walk according to the Spirit (Gal. 5:16; Eph. 5:18). This means that we, as those in Christ, must be intentional about cultivating our desires to know and enjoy God. We go to places and carve out time where we can meet with God and allow him to instruct us through his Word. We surround ourselves with brothers and sisters in Christ who will spur us on to good works, not tempting us to sin. We daily seek the Lord's provision through prayer (Eph. 6:18; 1 Thess. 5:17).

Eternity before Our Eyes

God has graciously given us in Scripture many examples of the lives of saints to encourage us toward purity. And he also uses ordinary men and women to inspire us. My (Grant's) dad, Charles Kelly Castleberry Jr., was a Marine Corps fighter pilot and a Christian. One night my dad's squadron took a "mandatory" trip to a beach house somewhere along the Atlantic Coast. No wives or children were allowed to come. This was a special night in which many of the young pilots would receive their "call signs." Shortly after my father arrived at the beach house, he realized why family members were not invited. Someone had invited strippers as entertainment for the evening. Later that night, when he confided this event to my mom, she asked him how he responded. He said that he had stayed in the corner of the beach house with his hand over his eyes.

A few months later, my father was killed in a midair collision over the Atlantic Ocean. After my father's crash, a pilot in the squadron gave my mom a picture that someone had taken inside the beach house that night. He told my mom that deep down "everyone respected Kelly for it, but no one had the guts to follow him." Sure enough, in the photo was my father in the corner, hand covering his eyes. When I was a young boy, my mom showed me that picture and explained the integrity and courage my dad had displayed in that moment—integrity and courage that had characterized his life in Christ. Mom framed the picture and put it in my room as a constant reminder of his legacy.

When the squadron cleaned out my dad's locker after the accident, they found taped up inside his locker Paul's last will and testament to a young pastor-in-training:

> For I am already being poured out as a drink offering, and the time of my departure has come. I have fought the good fight, I have finished the race, I have kept the faith. Henceforth there is laid up for me the crown of righteousness, which the Lord, the righteous judge, will award to me on that Day, and not only to me but also to all who have loved his appearing. (2 Tim. 4:6–8)

My dad covered his eyes at the beach house because they were fixed on his Savior. This focus isn't easy. As Paul said, it's a fight of faith. It's a fight for purity. But it's worth it. Christ is the purity we can count on. Keeping our eyes on him is worth it because he is the only one who can truly satisfy our souls. "For here we have no lasting city, but we seek the city that is to come" (Heb. 13:14).

12

My Recovery from Feminism

Courtney Reissig

Feminism. It's a word that elicits strong emotions from across the social spectrum. For some, it is a voice for the voiceless—the marginalized women of society who have been kept down far too long. For others, feminism is nothing more than a dirty word wielded by liberals and man-haters. And for still others, feminism is just one more way to say you believe in equality for women. *Feminism* is a loaded word if there ever was one.

Feminism began as a movement that sought a remedy for the inequality of the day. When first-wave feminism burst on the scene with Elizabeth Cady Stanton and others, women could not vote, hold property, or protect their children from the vicious circuit of child labor in factories. Women felt helpless as some of their husbands had rampant extramarital affairs while they, stranded housewives, had no avenue to seek help. Voting, in many ways, resolved those very real problems. But the movement morphed into second-wave feminism, which birthed the likes of Betty Friedan and

Gloria Steinem, who saw the stereotypical "happy housewife" of the 1950s and 1960s and thought women deserved better.

Fast-forward to today, and there's a third wave to feminism that has brought it into the mainstream. Feminism began as a push for equality and in many ways has now turned into a push beyond equality. It wasn't enough to be equal with a man; now women want to be better than men. It wasn't enough for women to be independent from men and their control; now women want to be above men in the home, workplace, and everywhere else. The birth of the feminist movement addressed real problems between men and women, but the grown child of the movement has moved on to other issues.

The battle of the sexes is alive and well.

Who Is a Feminist?

What do you think of when you hear the word *feminist*? Do you raise a fist in solidarity with this movement, which has spanned decades and opened countless doors for women? Or do you scoff, thinking that to be a feminist is to link arms in the bra-burning women's liberation movement your mother told stories about?

Regardless of what comes to mind, we can all probably think of someone we know, or know of, who typifies the feminist ideology. There are all types of fixtures of feminism, ranging from presidential candidates to evangelical scholars to college students—and I was one of them. Prior to conversion, I was the stereotypical Generation Y feminist—anti-marriage, anti–child rearing, a corporate-ladder hopeful. I couldn't imagine giving up my dreams and independence for a husband and children. I liked men and I liked kids; I was just afraid they would get in the way of *my* plans.

After conversion, I began to sing a slightly different tune, although I still held on to many of my previous ideals regarding marriage and settling down. I simply masked it with a missions/ministry focus, content to be the single girl on a mission to save a third-world country for Christ. Instead of really thinking through what the Bible has to say regarding marriage, children, and my goals in life, I just continued on my path of independence. I wanted to do "big things" for God. What's so wrong with that?

Feminism's Still Small Voice

What I did not want, or think I needed, was a changed life with changed priorities. It was not that I needed to find a husband or chuck any career aspirations. The problem was that I thought feminism was an outside-the-church issue, at least the conservative church to which I belonged. I had no notion that my heart, at its core, was fighting against the authority of God in the Scriptures (there's still a lot of change left to be done!). I didn't see that the feminism I clung to so tightly before Jesus saved me still had its tentacles tightly wrapped around my heart. It just wasn't obvious to me. I didn't understand feminism fully, and I most certainly didn't understand the far-reaching impact feminism has had on all of us. Feminism is so much a part of our culture that, as Mary Kassian so helpfully says in *The Feminist Mistake*, many of us are feminists and don't even know it.

How do I know this? I have seen it in my own life and in the lives of many of my friends. And it reveals itself in the subtlest ways. While I may have moved out of the militant feminist camp, I most certainly have been part of too many male bashing conversations in a dorm room or coffee shop with my girlfriends. You know the ones I'm talking about, right? The boyfriend dumps you or your best friend. The husband forgets to put the diaper on the baby before bed, *again*. The boss forgets an important meeting that you have worked all month preparing for. The pastor fails to recognize your situation. The fiancé doesn't understand the stress you are under as you prepare for the wedding of your dreams.

Regardless of the specifics, you and I have been in positions of frustration with men in our lives. And we probably have felt tempted to vent that frustration to our girlfriends—and by vent, I mean tear a guy down because he just can't seem to get his act together. *If only he were like me, then everything would be easier,* you think to yourself. And that, my friends, is feminism's still small voice speaking powerfully into your ear.

Recoiling from Authority

What we must understand about feminism is that it did not originate in the wake of the women's liberation movement of the 1970s. And the mother of feminism is actually far older than *Ms.* magazine and her friends. Feminism started in a garden somewhere in the Middle East thousands of years ago with someone named Eve.

Feminism expresses the very heart of a woman's fallen nature (as abusive headship or neglect of leadership is at the heart of male fallenness), manifesting itself in many different forms—from that frustration you feel rising when your husband asks you to trust him and you really don't want to (and think your way is better), to the more subtle heart attitude that thinks men don't really know what they are doing. Feminism is not just about equality for women—the Bible answers that question for us when God created Adam and Eve and called them both image bearers (Gen. 1:27). Feminism is about independence from rightful authority. And the truth is, we women are all feminists in need of recovery. It is not just about those who see themselves as feminists; it's also about those who can't see it in themselves.

An Overcoming Beauty

Recovering from feminism must start with embracing the gospel of our Lord Jesus Christ. Only then will we see the roots of feminism severed, because we will be clothed in the humility of Christ, who willingly submitted himself to the Father on our behalf. For older women, that will mean embracing and modeling femininity, motherhood, and marriage in a "Titus 2" way. For younger women, it will mean knowing the godly women in our congregations better than we know the celebrities on late-night television.

Feminist ideology is not confined to the brash Gloria Steinem types, or even the female executive with the corner office. Rather, it rises up in ordinary women in our congregations and homes, including the least obvious place: the mirror. Feminism is entrenched in our hearts apart from the saving work of Jesus, and not simply because we are militant against male authority, but primarily because we are opposed to the greatest authority of all: our Creator. The feminist is not some abstract "out there" woman. She is staring right at us every morning when we put on our makeup.

If we are going to make any headway in the gender discussion, we must first admit that our problem lies much deeper than in a woman filling the pulpit on Sunday morning, or in dads who shirk their responsibilities to their families. Our problem lies in the fact that there is no one righteous, and we are all opposed to God. We can't wake up one day and simply decide to be a Proverbs 31 woman any more than a man can wake up and decide to lead like Christ. Instead of seeing our gender differences as mere cultural constructions, we must first admit that there was something great going on in the garden—a *good* design—and when our first parents fell, it was distorted. In creating man and woman differently, God was pointing to the beauty of his Trinitarian fellowship and the relationship between Christ and his church. The fact that we fight against this beauty reveals our depravity even more.

Recovery for You and Me

Often we are so busy looking for the woman with the hyphenated name that we miss the woman who scoffs at a man for opening the door for her. I know that has been true for me. I have balked at the woman who chooses career over children, yet turned right around and berated my husband for not doing something the way I thought he should. Both of these actions are products of our feminist hearts. My "recovery" from feminism is not about learning how to bake pies, or my attempt to act more feminine (though these are often helpful things). Recovery is about repentance—repentance of my desire to be in control, to raise my fist against God's created order.

Only through repentance and faith in Christ am I—or anyone else, for that matter—able to renounce rebellion and gladly submit to the love of Jesus. It also means believing that God's Word regarding gender, and everything else, is true.

Recovery for many of us will also mean a reversal of the way we approach women in our congregations. It is no wonder so many young women don't desire motherhood when what they often hear from older women is "Get your degree first and live your life." And when I feel the judgment rising up in me at the sight of a young woman joyfully choosing marriage and family over a college degree, I realize that I still have a long way to go before this feminist is fully recovered.

But there is great hope. God has promised to complete the work in me that Jesus began (Phil. 1:6). From the time the first feminist, Eve, came on the scene until now, we have been in a cosmic battle against the flesh and Satan. The fallen world is at war against the image of Christ and his church, but not for long. Soon Jesus will consummate the great work accomplished in his cross and victory. Like all of our distortions of God's good design, feminism is defeated when the Seed crushes the Serpent (Gen. 3:15). And that's great news for recovering feminists like you and me.

13

Immature Manhood and the Hope of Something Better

Brandon Smith

I woke up on my best friend's apartment floor feeling like I had been hit by an eighteen wheeler. There's a scene in a popular movie in which the four main characters regain consciousness after a night of partying in Vegas. They sit up in the morning and survey their destroyed hotel room with utter amazement at chairs that were on fire, an overflowing hot tub, a tiger in the bathroom, and a chicken in the kitchen. They are concerned about what may or may not have happened the night before. In my real-life case, there wasn't any wildlife running around my friend's house, but we were in such a stupor that we half expected it.

It had been a rather routine night: alcohol, friends, and girls. We had gone drinking at a local bar that always had the best drink specials in town. For a bunch of college guys like us, two-dollar you-name-it drinks and a guaranteed chance of meeting girls was a no-brainer. Now, we were far from your average *Jersey Shore* or *Real World* crowd. We were not a wild and crazy bunch. We weren't known for our antics. We projected maturity. We had full-time jobs and never got into any serious legal trouble. Most of us even went to church together every Sunday. We were "relationship" kind of guys (sometimes). We were even committed to being accountability partners. But our veil of maturity was as durable as a wet piece of paper.

Immaturity 101

Immaturity is a subjective term. Some describe immaturity as singleness or living at home with parents or playing too many video games. Some say that immaturity is the inability to hold a steady job or earning poor grades in college. The scale is not the same for everyone, but it is not completely inexplicable. For our purposes here, it is best to describe immaturity by identifying its foundational theme: immature men shirk responsibility.

God gave Adam the great responsibility of stewarding creation. This is no small order. God charged him with working the garden, abstaining from the forbidden fruit of only one tree, naming animals, and joining together with his wife. When sin shattered the peaceful existence of Eden, Adam did not admit his guilt. He ran away. He hid from God. He quickly pointed the finger at Eve (Gen. 3:8–13).

The effects of sin are the same today—they merely reveal themselves in different ways. For example, Adam did not have an Xbox. This was not his temptation. But this is a real temptation for men today. Video games aren't the problem, though. I play video games on my cell phone, and so do most men I know. Are we immature? Are video games dangerous? Not necessarily. However, allowing video games to cut into actual responsibilities *is* a danger. If playing games interferes with the Lord's commands, leads to lack of productivity at work or school, or strains your relationships, there's an issue. Each person has his own levels of responsibility—no one is exempt. Instead of vilifying video games or joblessness or places of residence—or making excuses for them—we should be keenly aware of how these types of things might reflect our propensity to dodge our obligations.

As I said, I used to have the facade of maturity down pat, but that's just what it was—a facade. I looked like I had it all together, but I wasn't taking any of my responsibilities seriously. And I was looking everywhere but at the Man who would show me who I was meant to be.

Jesus: The Man among Men

It's easy to talk about what immaturity is and isn't. Anyone can point out flaws. The question remains, how is maturity possible?

We must start with the most profound truth in all of human history: "The Word became flesh and dwelt among us" (John 1:14). What does a mature man look like? Jesus Christ.

Jesus, the God-man without sin, modeled manhood perfectly. He yielded to God's will and prayed often (Matt. 11:25–26; 14:23). He was compassionate toward the lame and the sick (Matt. 8:13–14; 9:27–31). He defended those abused and rejected (Luke 7:36–50; John 8:3–11). He fought evil by casting out demons and rebuking Satan (Matt. 4:1–11; Mark 1:21–27; Luke 8:26–29).

Most importantly, he was radically sacrificial—sacrificial to the point of death, even death on a cross. In John 15:13, he tells his disciples that "greater love has no one than this, that someone lay down his life for his friends." This wasn't some pithy saying merely meant to encourage social justice. Jesus embodied this truth on the cross. He unflinchingly stared sin and death in the face, showing us his love.

He is worthy of worship because he is God, and he is worthy of imitation because he was God-centered in all he did on earth as a man. The aim of our lives is to look like Christ. Paul tells us to "put on the Lord Jesus Christ, and make no provision for the flesh, to gratify its desires" (Rom. 13:14), to love others as Christ loves us (Eph. 5:1–2), and to love our wives "as Christ loved the church and gave himself up for her" (Eph. 5:25).

So how is maturity possible? It's because by the power of the

Spirit, we no longer live but it is Christ who lives in us (Gal. 2:20). The past restraints of our infamous immaturity have been abolished. In Christ, sin will not have dominion over us. In Christ, we are free from condemnation. In Christ, we walk in the light. Though we'll never be perfect men on this side of eternity, we are forever united with the one perfect Man into whose image we are being conformed. Our hope is anchored in him alone. It isn't through our own righteousness that we become mature men, but only through the righteousness "which comes through faith in Christ, the righteousness from God that depends on faith" (Phil. 3:9).

The Crisis Moment

I once served with a pastor who said that many people have a "crisis moment" in which God radically changes their hearts. A sinful binge or a tragic moment can trigger a sudden awakening. While I know this is not a normative experience for everyone, this is certainly what happened to my friend and me that morning on his apartment floor.

Though it was not the first time we had indulged in rampant disregard for God, he used that night to expose the weight of our sins in a fresh way. He exploded our hearts, and we would never be the same. My friend went off to Bible college, and after many years of faithful church ministry, he is currently in the process of planting a church. I, too, ended up going to school to study the Bible and have been serving in ministry ever since. God never let us go.

To this day, my friend and I reflect on our deep understanding of Joseph's reminder to his brothers, "You meant evil against me, but God meant it for good" (Gen. 50:20). God used our evil as a means to turn our eyes off of ourselves and onto the beauty of his glorious grace. We were wrecking our lives, on a path in the opposite direction of anything to do with him. But he was actually drawing us in, targeting to transform our immature manhood—and our entire selves—into a work of grace. I was blind, and he gave me sight. I was sick, and he made me well. I was lost, and he gave me a compass.

Afterword

The Glad Conviction

Jonathan Parnell

John Ames was a dying man. But for this old Congregationalist pastor, the fictitious character of novelist Marilynne Robinson's *Gilead*, he knew his death would be soon—so soon, in fact, that he took up the task of leaving a memoir for his young son.

Writing from a quaint prairie town in Iowa, with the poetic nostalgia that makes sense coming from a man his age, Ames reflects on the plain beauty of this earth:

> So often I have seen the dawn come and the light flood over the land and everything turn radiant at once, that word "good" so profoundly affirmed in my soul that I am amazed I should be allowed to witness such a thing. There may have been a more wonderful first moment "when the morning stars sang together and all the sons of God shouted for joy," but for all I know to the contrary, they still do sing and shout, and they certainly might well.[1]

---

[1] Marilynne Robinson, *Gilead: A Novel* (New York: Picador, 2004), 246.

It is a wonderful thing to feel what Ames feels here. It's wonderful to have moments when we reflect upon this place, when we see beyond the sin-smeared canvas into the vibrancy of life that teems along the simplest sunrise. It's wonderful to remember that this all came from nothing, spoken into existence by the God who needs no one, the God who looked at everything he made and called it good.

It's wonderful when, like Ames, we sense that word *good* so profoundly affirmed in our souls that we are amazed we should be allowed to witness such a thing. And not only witness, but even more amazing, we get to participate in that goodness. We live in a world that is deep and glorious in a trillion ways, and at the center, by God's design, *there we are* as men and women created in his image. There are no *ordinary* people, as C. S. Lewis reminds us. *God made us.* He made us like him—as men and women—to share in his beauty, to enjoy his glory, to reflect his worth.

And perhaps that point is the place to close this book on Christian complementarity.

That Good Song

The beauty, the glory, the honor—that is the angle I took in a recent imaginary conversation. My pretend dialogue, confined though it was to my own head, was instigated by a speaker I heard at a recent conference. The topic was content strategy on the web, and the woman doing the talking was a respected author and guru in this particular field. She had brilliant insights about online trends, shared key lessons learned, offered memorable one-liners, and somehow managed to bring up "sexism" at least four times. Her topic had little, if anything, to do with gender, but it became clear that she had been the victim of mistreatment in the past. Her references to gender equality became so prevalent, in fact, that in certain asides it could have passed as a women's empowerment rally.

Meanwhile, I was wondering how I would explain biblical complementarity to someone who, by past experiences and projected misconceptions, thinks the idea of distinctive gender roles is utterly backwater, even immoral. I felt like I knew about something beautiful she had never seen or heard. So I wondered, still jotting down notes and gleaning what I could, how in the world might I explain Christian complementarity to a woman like her? That's how the conversation started with this talented female professional from Silicon Valley.

SV: So, what is that you call your belief about men and women? Comple-*what*?

JP: Complementarity. I know, it doesn't exactly roll off your tongue. But the vision makes sense for what the Bible teaches about humanity as men and women. *Complement* is the word. If you prefer, we could call it the harmony of manhood and womanhood.

SV: Harmony. Okay, what does that mean?

JP: God is at the center. We Christians believe, as the Bible shows us, that he created everything. And at the pinnacle of his creation was humankind in two distinct genders: male and female. Both men and women were set apart from everything else in the world with the special dignity of bearing God's own image, which means we "image" God in his world in a unique way, as his special representatives. We get to share in some of the same work he does—work like creating and stewarding and exercising oversight. As you alluded to in your session, men and women have an amazing capacity to build and innovate. We have this wonderful ability to make really good things. I believe God gave us this gift. He gave it to both men and women. And not only that, the reason he gave us this gift is for our happiness. He created us to experience eternal joy, to be glad in who he is and in all the expressions of his worth.

SV: So what does this have to do with harmony?

JP: Well, we Christians believe that inherent to this purpose of joy in God is the fact that he made two different kinds of humans, one male and one female. And because these differences are not happenstance, but integral to his design, there is something about these differences that maximizes our joy. Like music, biblical complementarity, or the harmony of manhood and womanhood, says that something more enjoyable happens when different parts work together as one, a kind of unity in diversity.

SV: What does this mean for women?

JP: It means for women what it does for men. We see this most vividly in marriage—which Jesus said is a man and woman becoming "one flesh" (Matt. 19:5)—but the differences apply to men and women in general, too. It means there is one song, but it has two different parts. It means that the woman has one sound and the man has another. Neither sound is greater or more important than the other. In fact, you must have both sounds to get the song. The whole is greater than the sum of the parts.

SV: What part does the woman play, then?

JP: Without the woman's part, there's no real music. It's so important—just as important as the man's. To oversimplify it, her role in marriage, which relates to femininity in general, is one of affirmation, nurture, and trust toward her husband.

SV: Wait, what does the man do?

JP: Again, to oversimplify, his role, complementary to the woman's, is one of leadership, provision, and protection toward his wife, and more generally, toward all women and children. In other words, when the ship is sinking, men don't jump on the lifeboats first.

SV: No thanks. Women can lead and provide and protect better than most men I know.

JP: I don't doubt it. The roles are not regulated by competency, though. It's about the music, about playing your different parts together to make the song. And of course, it doesn't mean that women never do those things. Yes, women lead and provide and protect in many ways every day, just like men affirm and nurture and trust. The focus though, as it's seen most clearly in marriage, has to do with the husband's and wife's relation to one another for the sake of the music. To make that music, the husband steps out first in leading, and the wife affirms his initiative in doing so. *Two parts, one song.* The husband takes up the mantle of provision, of figuring out how to holistically care for his family along with her help, and the wife nurtures that instinct and strategy. *Two parts, one song.* The husband—just like Jesus did when he died for his church—always leans forward in the face of sacrifice, in the name of love, and the wife, in the safety of that love, trusts him. *Two parts, one song.*

SV: And this is about joy?

JP: Yes, that's exactly right. That song is part of the joy God created us to know. He made us to shine for him and enjoy him. Sin messed that up, distorting our sense of purpose and our relationship to God. And that's why Jesus came: to die for the sins of men and women, to conquer death for our sake and restore our relationship to God and the everlasting joy we were meant to experience in him—the joy we were meant to experience as men and women, created equal in his image to play two different parts of one great song.

SV: So I'll admit that is interesting.

JP: I think so, too. I realize that this song, or this harmony as we're calling it, isn't something you hear a lot about. Or maybe, because of bad experiences in the past, you immediately read "differences" to mean "inequality." But that's not the case. I'm right there with you renouncing anything that demeans the God-given dignity of women. Christians don't advocate one gender over another; we value both for the sake of the song. And I believe that you, like every woman and man, were designed to make music like this. I believe it will resonate deep down with who God made you as a woman, and perhaps, if he will give you the ears, one day you'll hear this song and sense that word *good* profoundly affirmed in your soul.

Contributors

Denny Burk is associate professor of biblical studies and ethics at Boyce College, the undergraduate arm of The Southern Baptist Theological Seminary. He also serves as associate pastor at Kenwood Baptist Church in Louisville, Kentucky. He is the author of *What Is the Meaning of Sex?* (2013), and a contributor to several books and journals. He and his wife, Susan, have four children.

GraceAnna Castleberry is a wife, mother, and worker at home. She lives in Louisville, Kentucky, with her husband, Grant. She formerly worked for Cru at Duke University, leading women's Bible studies. She and her mother host a weekly radio program, *Mothering from the Heart*, on WAGP.net. GraceAnna is a contributor to the Council on Biblical Manhood and Womanhood and blogs regularly at graceannacastleberry.com.

Grant Castleberry is the executive director of the Council on Biblical Manhood and Womanhood. He is an officer in the Marine Corps, having served as an air traffic control officer and as a series commander at Marine Corps Recruit Depot Parris Island. He and GraceAnna have two young daughters.

Christina Fox is a licensed counselor and a regular contributor to various websites and publications, including desiringGod.org, the Gospel Coalition, and the Council on Biblical Manhood and Womanhood. She and her husband reside in sunny South Florida with their two boys, whom she homeschools.

Gloria Furman is a wife, mother of four, and cross-cultural worker. Her family has lived in the United Arab Emirates since 2008, where her husband, Dave, pastors Redeemer Church of Dubai. Gloria is the author of *Glimpses of Grace: Treasuring the Gospel in Your Home* (2013) and *Treasuring Christ When Your Hands Are Full: Gospel Meditations for Busy Moms* (2014). She blogs at gloria furman.com.

David Mathis is executive editor at desiringGod.org, pastor at Cities Church in Minneapolis–Saint Paul, and adjunct professor at Bethlehem College and Seminary. He writes regularly at desiring God.org and is coauthor of *How to Stay Christian in Seminary* (2014), and coeditor with John Piper of *Acting the Miracle* (2013); *Finish the Mission* (2012); *Thinking. Loving. Doing.* (2011); and *With Calvin in the Theater of God* (2010). David and his wife, Megan, have three children.

Andy Naselli is assistant professor of New Testament and biblical theology at Bethlehem College and Seminary, research manager for D. A. Carson, and administrator of *Themelios*. He also writes regularly at andynaselli.com. Andy and his wife, Jenni, have three daughters.

Trillia Newbell is the author of *United: Captured by God's Vision of Diversity* (2014). Her writings on issues of faith, family, and diversity are regularly featured online. She currently is the consultant on women's initiatives for the Ethics and Religious Liberty Commission for the Southern Baptist Convention and lead editor of *Karis*, a blog for the Council on Biblical Manhood and Womanhood. She is married to her best friend and love, Thern. They reside with their two children near Nashville, Tennessee.

Jonathan Parnell is a writer and content strategist at desiringGod .org, and is the lead pastor of Cities Church in Minneapolis–Saint Paul, where he lives with his wife, Melissa, and their five children. He is also the coauthor of *How to Stay Christian in Seminary* (2014).

Tony Reinke is a staff writer for desiringGod.org, host of the *Ask Pastor John* podcast, and author of *Lit! A Christian Guide to Reading Books* (2011) and *Newton on the Christian Life: To Live Is Christ* (2015). He lives in Minneapolis with his wife and three children.

Courtney Reissig is a pastor's wife, mother, and writer. She is the author of *The Accidental Feminist: Restoring Our Delight in God's Good Design* (2015). Courtney and her husband live in Little Rock, Arkansas, with their twin boys.

Joe Rigney is assistant professor of theology and Christian worldview at Bethlehem College and Seminary, and the author of *Live Like a Narnian: Christian Discipleship in Lewis's Chronicles* (2013). He lives in Minneapolis with his wife and two sons.

Marshall Segal is executive assistant to John Piper for desiringGod .org and writes regularly for their site. Unmarried, he lives in Minneapolis and serves and worships at Bethlehem Baptist Church.

Brandon Smith serves in leadership and teaches theology and church history at Criswell College, where he is also associate editor of the *Criswell Theological Review*. He recently edited the book *Make, Mature, Multiply* and writes regularly at Patheos. He is proud to be Christa's husband and Harper Grace's daddy.

Owen Strachan is married to Bethany and the father of three children. He is the president of the Council on Biblical Manhood and Womanhood, assistant professor of Christian theology and church history at The Southern Baptist Theological Seminary and Boyce College, and director of the Carl F. H. Henry Institute for Evangelical Engagement at SBTS. He is the author of *Risky Gospel: Abandon Fear and Build Something Awesome* (2013).

General Index

Scripture Index